Common Core Mastery
Reading Paired Text

Grade **1**

The following images were provided through Shutterstock.com and are protected by copyright:

vita khorzhevska, Kisialiou Yury, Iryna Rasko, Menna, Igor Strukov, Dudarev Mikhail (page 88); INSAGO, Olga_Anourina (page 89); David Salcedo (pages 89, 91); Eric Isselee, oksana2010 (page 90); Olga_Anourina, INSAGO (page 91); swissmacky, worldswildlifewonders, gumbao, Madlen, Mogens Trolle, Piotr Rzeszutek (page 96); Eric Isselee, defpicture, Iakov Filimonov (page 97); Ultrashock, Alexander Cherednichenko (page 98); Ultrashock (page 99); Georgios Kollidas (pages 135, 137); Oleg Golovnev (pages 135, 136, 137, 139); Rob Byron, Aleks vF, Pasko Maksim, rvlsoft, Blend Images, Ramona Kaulitzki (page 156); Catherine Wong (pages 157, 159); iTunes_iRead Monthly (page 158); Hung Chung Chih, Vasilius (page 159)

Editorial Development: Marti Beeck
    Lisa Vitarisi Mathews
Copy Editing: Anna Pelligra
Art Direction: Cheryl Puckett
Cover Design: Yuki Meyer
Cover Illustration: Chris Vallo
Illustration: Ann Iosa
Design/Production: Susan Lovell
    Jessica Onken
Art & Photo Management: Kathy Kopp

EMC 1371

Evan-Moor®
Helping Children Learn

Visit
teaching-standards.com
to view a correlation
of this book.
This is a free service.

*Correlated to State and
Common Core State Standards*

Congratulations on your purchase of some of the finest teaching materials in the world.

Photocopying the pages in this book is permitted for <u>single-classroom use only</u>. Making photocopies for additional classes or schools is prohibited.

Contents

Correlations
Common Core State Standards

	Science Selections							
RL **Reading Standards for Literature, Grade 1**	Jacob's Arm	How Bones Work	Are the Moon and the Sun the Same?	Earth's Moon	What Is Matter?	Wonderful Water	Goats	Wild About Food
Key Ideas and Details								
1.1 Ask and answer questions about key details in a text.	•	•	•	•	•	•	•	•
1.2 Retell stories, including key details, and demonstrate understanding of their central message or lesson.	•							
1.3 Describe characters, settings, and major events in a story, using key details.	•							
Craft and Structure								
1.4 Identify words and phrases in stories or poems that suggest feelings or appeal to the senses.	•		•	•	•	•	•	•
1.5 Explain major differences between books that tell stories and books that give information, drawing on a wide reading of a range of text types.	•	•						
Integration of Knowledge and Ideas								
1.7 Use illustrations and details in a story to describe its characters, setting, or events.	•	•	•	•	•	•	•	•
Range of Reading and Level of Text Complexity								
1.10 With prompting and support, read prose and poetry of appropriate complexity for grade 1.	•	•	•	•	•	•	•	•

W **Writing Standards, Grade 1**								
Text Types and Purposes								
1.2 Write informative/explanatory texts in which they name a topic, supply some facts about the topic, and provide some sense of closure.	•	•	•	•			•	•
1.8 With guidance and support from adults, recall information from experiences or gather information from provided sources to answer a question.	•	•	•	•	•	•	•	•

Correlations
Common Core State Standards

Social Studies Selections							
My Country 'Tis of Thee	A Flag for America	The Wonder of Art	A Day in the Country	Ideas and Inventions	Ben Franklin	**RL**	**Reading Standards for Literature, Grade 1**
							Key Ideas and Details
●	●	●	●	●	●		**1.1** Ask and answer questions about key details in a text.
	●	●	●	●	●		**1.2** Retell stories, including key details, and demonstrate understanding of their central message or lesson.
	●	●	●	●	●		**1.3** Describe characters, settings, and major events in a story, using key details.
							Craft and Structure
●	●	●	●	●	●		**1.4** Identify words and phrases in stories or poems that suggest feelings or appeal to the senses.
		●	●				**1.5** Explain major differences between books that tell stories and books that give information, drawing on a wide reading of a range of text types.
							Integration of Knowledge and Ideas
●	●	●	●	●	●		**1.7** Use illustrations and details in a story to describe its characters, setting, or events.
							Range of Reading and Level of Text Complexity
●	●	●	●	●	●		**1.10** With prompting and support, read prose and poetry of appropriate complexity for grade 1.

My Country 'Tis of Thee	A Flag for America	The Wonder of Art	A Day in the Country	Ideas and Inventions	Ben Franklin	**W**	**Writing Standards, Grade 1**
							Text Types and Purposes
●	●	●	●	●	●		**1.2** Write informative/explanatory texts in which they name a topic, supply some facts about the topic, and provide some sense of closure.
●	●	●	●	●	●		**1.8** With guidance and support from adults, recall information from experiences or gather information from provided sources to answer a question.

Correlations
Common Core State Standards

	Science Selections							
RIT **Reading Standards for Informational Text, Grade 1**	Jacob's Arm (fiction)	How Bones Work	Are the Moon and the Sun the Same?	Earth's Moon	What Is Matter?	Wonderful Water	Goats	Wild About Food
Key Ideas and Details								
1.1 Ask and answer questions about key details in a text.		●	●	●	●	●	●	●
1.2 Identify the main topic and retell key details of a text.		●	●	●	●	●	●	●
1.3 Describe the connection between two individuals, events, ideas, or pieces of information in a text.		●	●	●	●	●	●	●
Craft and Structure								
1.4 Ask and answer questions to help determine or clarify the meaning of words and phrases in a text.		●	●	●	●	●	●	●
1.6 Distinguish between information provided by pictures or other illustrations and information provided by the words in a text.		●	●	●	●	●	●	●
Integration of Knowledge and Ideas								
1.7 Use the illustrations and details in a text to describe its characters, setting, or events.		●	●	●	●	●	●	●
1.8 Identify the reasons an author gives to support points in a text.		●	●	●	●	●	●	●
1.9 Identify basic similarities in and differences between two texts on the same topic (e.g., in illustrations, descriptions, or procedures).	●	●	●	●	●	●	●	●
Range of Reading and Level of Text Complexity								
1.10 With prompting and support, read informational texts appropriately complex for grade 1.		●	●	●	●	●	●	●

Correlations
Common Core State Standards

Social Studies Selections							Reading Standards for Informational Text, Grade 1
My Country 'Tis of Thee	A Flag for America	The Wonder of Art	A Day in the Country (fiction)	Ideas and Inventions	Ben Franklin	**RIT**	
							Key Ideas and Details
●	●	●		●	●		**1.1** Ask and answer questions about key details in a text.
●	●	●		●	●		**1.2** Identify the main topic and retell key details of a text.
●	●	●		●	●		**1.3** Describe the connection between two individuals, events, ideas, or pieces of information in a text.
							Craft and Structure
●	●	●		●	●		**1.4** Ask and answer questions to help determine or clarify the meaning of words and phrases in a text.
●	●	●		●	●		**1.6** Distinguish between information provided by pictures or other illustrations and information provided by the words in a text.
							Integration of Knowledge and Ideas
●	●	●		●	●		**1.7** Use the illustrations and details in a text to describe its characters, setting, or events.
●	●	●		●	●		**1.8** Identify the reasons an author gives to support points in a text.
●	●	●	●	●	●		**1.9** Identify basic similarities in and differences between two texts on the same topic (e.g., in illustrations, descriptions, or procedures).
							Range of Reading and Level of Text Complexity
●	●	●		●	●		**1.10** With prompting and support, read informational texts appropriately complex for grade 1.

Correlations
Texas Essential Knowledge and Skills

110.13. English Language Arts and Reading, Grade 1	Science Selections					
	Jacob's Arm	How Bones Work	Are the Moon and the Sun the Same?	Earth's Moon	What Is Matter?	Wonderful Water
Reading						
(5) Reading/Fluency. Students read grade-level text with fluency and comprehension. Students are expected to read aloud grade-level appropriate text with fluency (rate, accuracy, expression, appropriate phrasing) and comprehension.	●	●	●	●	●	●
(6C) Reading/Vocabulary Development. Students understand new vocabulary and use it when reading and writing. Students are expected to determine what words mean from how they are used in a sentence, either heard or read.	●	●	●	●	●	●
(13) Reading/Comprehension of Informational Text/Culture and History. Students analyze, make inferences and draw conclusions about the author's purpose in cultural, historical, and contemporary contexts and provide evidence from the text to support their understanding. Students are expected to identify the topic and explain the author's purpose in writing about the text.						
(14A, B, C, D) Reading/Comprehension of Informational Text/Expository Text. Students analyze, make inferences and draw conclusions about expository text and provide evidence from text to support their understanding. Students are expected to: restate the main idea, heard or read; identify important facts or details in text, heard or read; retell the order of events in a text by referring to the words and/or illustrations; and use text features (e.g., title, tables of contents, illustrations) to locate specific information in text.		●	●	●	●	●
Writing						
(19A, C) Writing/Expository and Procedural Texts. Students write expository and procedural or work-related texts to communicate ideas and information to specific audiences for specific purposes. Students are expected to: write brief compositions about topics of interest to the student; write brief comments on literary or informational texts.	●	●	●	●	●	●

Correlations
Texas Essential Knowledge and Skills

			Social Studies Selections				
Goats	Wild About Food	My Country 'Tis of Thee	A Flag for America	The Wonder of Art	A Day in the Country	Ideas and Inventions	Ben Franklin
•	•	•	•	•	•	•	•
•	•	•	•	•	•	•	•
		•	•	•		•	•
•	•		•	•	•	•	•
•	•	•	•	•	•	•	•

How to Use

Reading Paired Text contains reading selections about grade-level science and social studies topics. The supporting comprehension and writing activities use Common Core methodology to guide students to closely examine the texts, discuss the topic, and ultimately improve their reading comprehension. The pairing of texts allows students to compare multiple viewpoints and provides opportunities to integrate information.

Each unit contains two thematically related selections (minibooks or two-page texts) that are focused around a Big Question. Each selection's activities include vocabulary development in context, an oral close reading discussion, comprehension questions, and a writing prompt. The unit assessment includes discussion of the topic, texts, and Big Question, as well as a writing prompt.

Unit Overview

The unit title, the student objective, and the Big Question are presented.

TOPIC INTRODUCTION
Background information connects students to the topic without giving away the selection content.

PAIRED TEXT SELECTIONS
Under each selection, genre and Guided Reading Levels (D–H) are listed, as well as teacher pages and student activities.

ASSESSMENT MATERIALS
Activities at the end of the unit help students compare and integrate what they have learned about the topic.

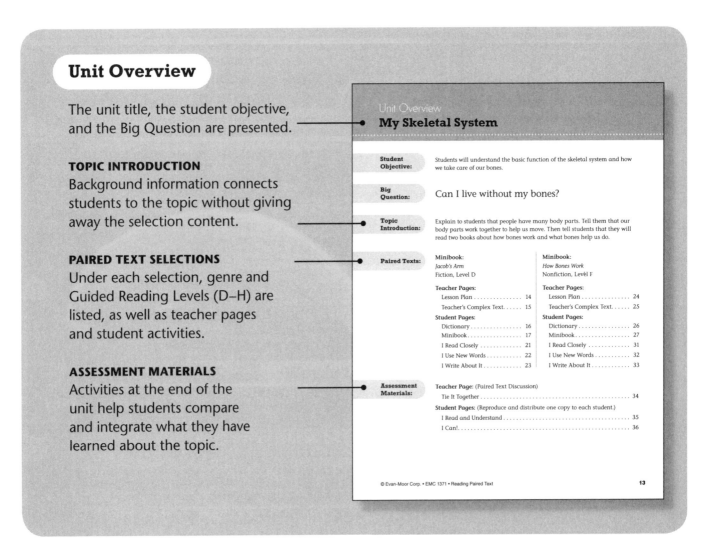

Teacher Pages

LESSON PLAN

The suggested teaching path guides you through each selection and related activities. It also provides selection-related background information for students to access before reading.

TEACHER'S COMPLEX TEXT

Students listen to the Teacher's Complex Text read aloud. It includes complex ideas and content vocabulary that is above first-grade reading level. Additional facts and details about the topic also increase students' comprehensive understanding of the topic.

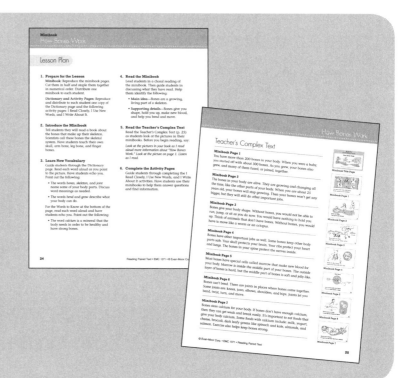

Student Pages

DICTIONARY

A picture dictionary provides visual information and helps connect words with meanings. Additional vocabulary is introduced in a Words to Know list.

SELECTIONS

Students read two minibooks or selections about the unit topic. They learn information from the texts as well as the illustrations, photos, and graphics. They use information from both texts to develop their body of knowledge about the topic and to acquire content vocabulary.

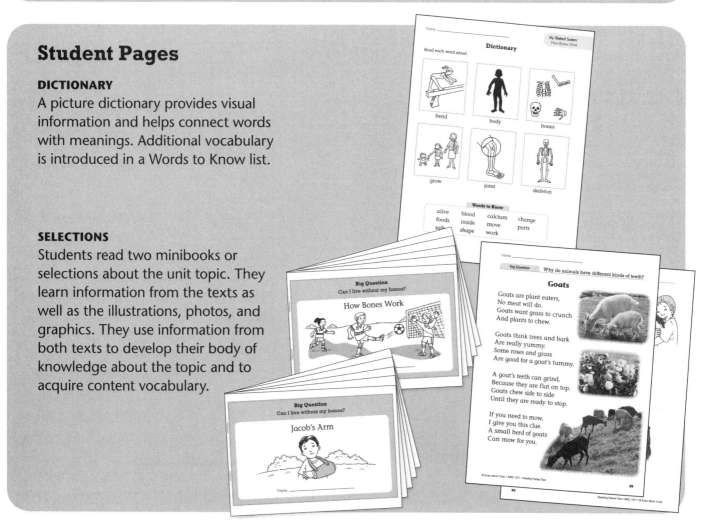

Student Pages, continued

I READ CLOSELY

A close reading activity presents students with pictures and sentences that ask them to connect text meaning and picture meaning.

I USE NEW WORDS

Students practice applying vocabulary by completing sentences with the appropriate vocabulary word.

I WRITE ABOUT IT

Students further show what they have learned by writing. They use ideas and details they have read to respond to a text-based writing prompt.

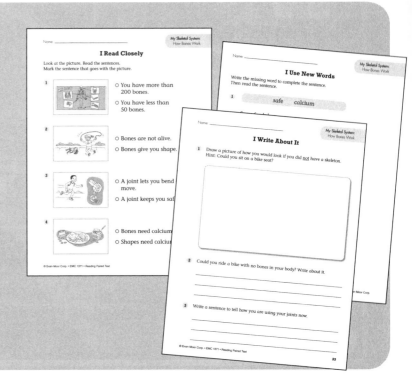

Assessment Materials

Teacher Page

TIE IT TOGETHER

Oral discussion questions tie together how both selections relate to the unit topic and the Big Question.

Student Pages

I READ AND UNDERSTAND

A reading comprehension activity asks students to answer questions about the selections, prompting them to think about and compare details.

I CAN!

Students will organize details and synthesize ideas into a written response to show understanding of both selections.

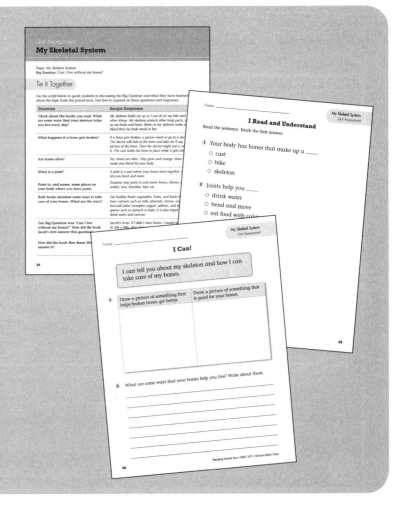

My Skeletal System

Student Objective: Students will understand the basic function of the skeletal system and how we take care of our bones.

Big Question:

Can I live without my bones?

Topic Introduction: Explain to students that people have many body parts. Tell them that our body parts work together to help us move. Then tell students that they will read two books about how bones work and what bones help us do.

Paired Texts:

<table>
<tr><td>

Minibook:

Jacob's Arm

Fiction, Level D
</td><td>

Minibook:

How Bones Work

Nonfiction, Level F
</td></tr>
</table>

Assessment Materials:

Lesson Plan

1. Prepare for the Lesson

Minibook: Reproduce the minibook pages. Cut them in half and staple them together in numerical order. Distribute one minibook to each student.

Dictionary and Activity Pages: Reproduce and distribute to each student one copy of the Dictionary page and the following activity pages: I Read Closely, I Use New Words, and I Write About It.

2. Introduce the Minibook

Begin the lesson by having students feel the bones in their arms. Have them bend their elbows and feel the muscles around their arm bones. Tell them that they will read a book about a boy who breaks his arm bone while riding his bike.

3. Learn New Vocabulary

Guide students through the Dictionary page. Read each word aloud as you point to the picture. Have students echo you. Point out the following:

- An *X-ray* is a special kind of photograph that shows the inside of a person's body.

For the Words to Know at the bottom of the page, read each word aloud and have students echo you. Point out the following:

- Words like *boom* and *crash* imitate sounds.

- In this book, the word *rest* means "to stay still; to sit or lie down."

- In this book, the word *ride* means "to sit on something that is moving."

4. Read the Minibook

Lead students in a choral reading of the minibook. Then guide students in discussing what they have read. Help them identify the following:

- **Main idea**—When Jacob breaks his arm, it affects his whole body.

- **Supporting details**—Jacob needs to wear a cast on his arm and stop riding his bike until his arm heals. Jacob takes care of his body while he is healing.

5. Read the Teacher's Complex Text

Read the Teacher's Complex Text (p. 15) as students look at the pictures in their minibooks. Before you begin reading, say:

Look at the pictures in your book as I read aloud more information about "Jacob's Arm." Look at the picture on page 1. Listen as I read.

6. Complete the Activity Pages

Guide students through completing the I Read Closely, I Use New Words, and I Write About It activities. Have students use their minibooks to help them answer questions and find information.

Teacher's Complex Text

Minibook Title Page

Minibook Page 1

One day, Jacob was riding his bike. All of a sudden, there was a boom, and a crash! Jacob was on the ground, with his bike on top of him. He tried to get up. "Ouch!" he cried. His arm hurt a lot!

Minibook Page 1

Minibook Page 2

Jacob and his mom went straight to see Dr. Beck. The doctor looked at Jacob's arm. "Hmmm...," he said. "We need to check your arm bones." A big machine took a picture of the bones inside Jacob's arm. The picture is called an X-ray. Dr. Beck looked at the X-ray and said, "Your arm bone broke when you fell. I'm glad you wore your helmet. It helped protect your brain."

Minibook Page 2

Minibook Page 3

Then Dr. Beck put a cast on Jacob's arm to hold the broken bone in place. "It will take about 6 weeks for your arm to heal," he said. "The cast will protect your bone and muscle parts while they get better." Dr. Beck told Jacob that his body needed healthy food and plenty of water. He would need to rest his arm, but he could get exercise by going for walks.

Minibook Page 3

Minibook Page 4

Jacob took good care of his body. He ate healthy foods, including a lot of fresh vegetables and fruits. Jacob drank plenty of water. His body got all the important nutritional energy that it needed to get better.

Minibook Page 4

Minibook Page 5

Jacob and his big brother went for a walk every day. Exercise helped all his body parts stay healthy while his arm got better. The walking exercise also helped him feel good and sleep well at night.

Minibook Page 5

Minibook Page 6

Even though he missed riding his bike, Jacob let his arm rest and heal. Slowly it started to feel better. Jacob knew that helping his arm heal would help his whole body feel better, too.

Minibook Page 6

Minibook Page 7

Six weeks went by. Dr. Beck told Jacob that he had taken good care of himself, and it was time to take off the cast. Jacob could finally ride his bike again. He made sure to always wear his bike helmet!

Minibook Page 7

Name: _____

Dictionary

Read each word aloud.

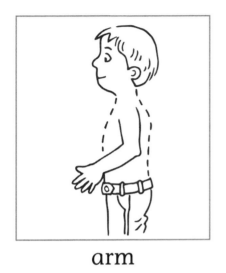

arm

bike

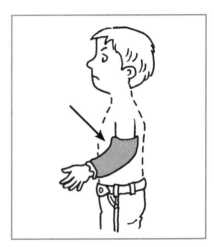

cast

drank

healthy food

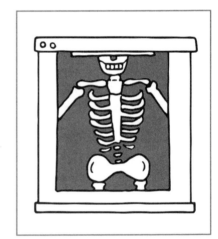

X-ray

Words to Know

bone	boom	broken	crash
himself	hurt	ouch	rest
ride	water	weeks	

Jacob's Arm

Name: _____

Boom, crash, ouch!
Jacob fell off his bike.
His arm hurt a lot!

1

Dr. Beck looked at an X-ray of Jacob's arm.
His arm bone was broken.

2

Dr. Beck put a cast on Jacob's arm.
He told Jacob how to take care of himself.

3

Jacob ate healthy food.
He drank a lot of water.

4

Jacob went for a walk every day.
He got a lot of rest, too.

5

Jacob wanted to ride his bike.
It looked like fun.

Six weeks went by.
Jacob's arm was better.
Then he could ride his bike again.

Name: _____

I Read Closely

Look at the picture. Read the sentences.
Mark the sentence that goes with the picture.

1

○ Jacob fell off his bike.

○ Jacob went for a walk.

2

○ Jacob's mom put a cast on his arm.

○ Dr. Beck put a cast on Jacob's arm.

3

○ Jacob ate healthy food.

○ Jacob got a lot of rest.

4

○ It took ten weeks for Jacob's arm to get better.

○ It took six weeks for Jacob's arm to get better.

I Use New Words

Write the missing word to complete the sentence.
Then read the sentence.

1   X-ray   ouch

An _____ can show a broken bone.

2   rest   ride

You can _____ a bike.

3   weeks   water

We drank _____.

4   healthy   broken

I feel good when I eat _____ food.

5   crash   arm

I have a cast on my _____.

I Write About It

1   Draw a picture to show what Jacob did to help his arm get better.

2   Write about your picture.

_____

_____

_____

_____

_____

_____

Lesson Plan

1. Prepare for the Lesson

Minibook: Reproduce the minibook pages. Cut them in half and staple them together in numerical order. Distribute one minibook to each student.

Dictionary and Activity Pages: Reproduce and distribute to each student one copy of the Dictionary page and the following activity pages: I Read Closely, I Use New Words, and I Write About It.

2. Introduce the Minibook

Tell students they will read a book about the bones that make up their skeleton. Scientists call these bones the skeletal system. Have students touch their own skull, arm bone, leg bone, and finger bones.

3. Learn New Vocabulary

Guide students through the Dictionary page. Read each word aloud as you point to the picture. Have students echo you. Point out the following:

- The words *bones, skeleton,* and *joint* name some of your body parts. Discuss word meanings as needed.

- The words *bend* and *grow* describe what your body can do.

For the Words to Know at the bottom of the page, read each word aloud and have students echo you. Point out the following:

- The word *calcium* is a mineral that the body needs in order to be healthy and have strong bones.

4. Read the Minibook

Lead students in a choral reading of the minibook. Then guide students in discussing what they have read. Help them identify the following:

- **Main idea**—Bones are a growing, living part of a skeleton.

- **Supporting details**—Bones give you shape, hold you up, make new blood, and help you bend and move.

5. Read the Teacher's Complex Text

Read the Teacher's Complex Text (p. 25) as students look at the pictures in their minibooks. Before you begin reading, say:

Look at the pictures in your book as I read aloud more information about "How Bones Work." Look at the picture on page 1. Listen as I read.

6. Complete the Activity Pages

Guide students through completing the I Read Closely, I Use New Words, and I Write About It activities. Have students use their minibooks to help them answer questions and find information.

Teacher's Complex Text

Minibook Page 1

You have more than 200 bones in your body. When you were a baby, you started off with about 300 bones. As you grew, your bones also grew, and many of them fused, or joined, together.

Minibook Page 2

The bones in your body are alive. They are growing and changing all the time, like the other parts of your body. When you are about 25 years old, your bones will stop growing. Then your bones won't get any bigger, but they will still do other important jobs.

Minibook Page 3

Bones give your body shape. Without bones, you would not be able to run, jump, or sit as you do now. You would have nothing to hold you up. Think of animals that don't have bones. Without bones, you would have to move like a worm or an octopus.

Minibook Page 4

Bones have other important jobs as well. Some bones keep other body parts safe. Your skull protects your brain. Your ribs protect your heart and lungs. The bones in your spine protect the nerves inside.

Minibook Page 5

Most bones have special cells called marrow that make new blood for your body. Marrow is inside the middle part of your bones. The outside layer of bones is hard, but the middle part of bones is soft and jelly-like.

Minibook Page 6

Bones can't bend. There are joints in places where bones come together. Some joints are: knees, jaws, elbows, shoulders, and hips. Joints let you bend, twist, turn, and move.

Minibook Page 7

Bones store calcium for your body. If bones don't have enough calcium, then they can get weak and break easily. It's important to eat foods that give your body calcium. Some foods with calcium include: milk, yogurt, cheese, broccoli, dark leafy greens like spinach and kale, almonds, and salmon. Exercise also helps keep bones strong.

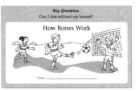

Minibook Title Page

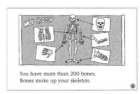

Minibook Page 1

Minibook Page 2

Minibook Page 3

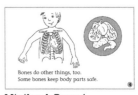

Minibook Page 4

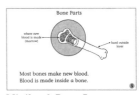

Minibook Page 5

Minibook Page 6

Minibook Page 7

Dictionary

Read each word aloud.

bend

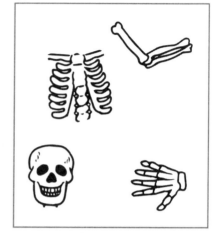

body

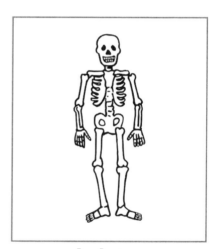

bones

grow

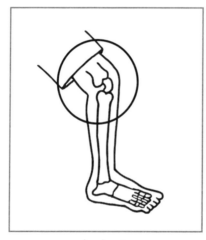

joint

skeleton

Words to Know

alive	blood	calcium	change
foods	inside	move	parts
safe	shape	work	

Reading Paired Text • EMC 1371 • © Evan-Moor Corp.

How Bones Work

Name: _____

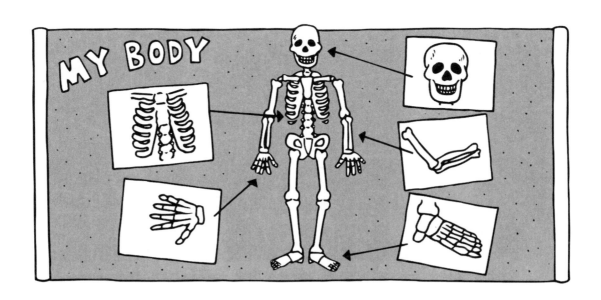

You have more than 200 bones.
Bones make up your skeleton.

1

Bones are alive.
They grow and change.

2

Bones give you shape.
They help you run, jump, and sit.

3

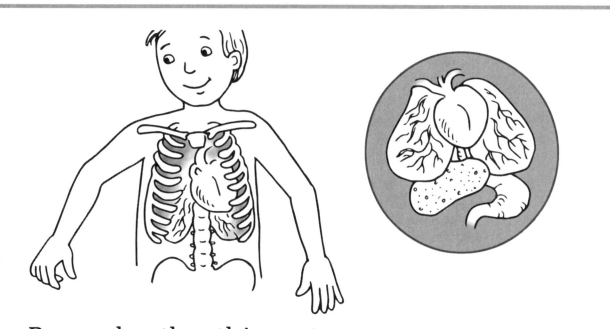

Bones do other things, too.
Some bones keep body parts safe.

4

Bone Parts

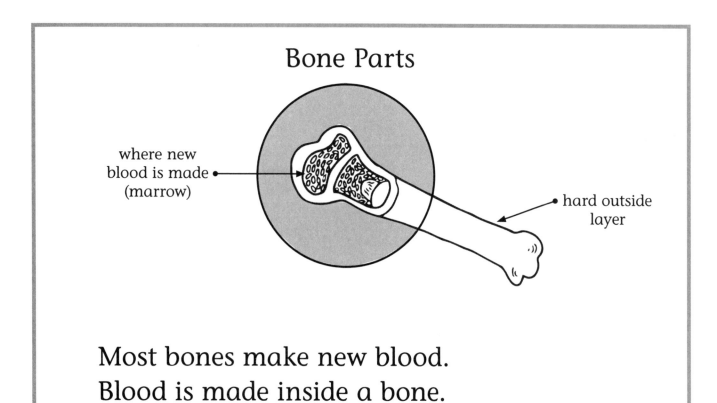

where new blood is made (marrow)

hard outside layer

Most bones make new blood.
Blood is made inside a bone.

5

Bones meet at a joint.
A joint lets you bend and move.

6

Bones need calcium.
It is good to eat foods that have calcium.

7

Name: _____

I Read Closely

Look at the picture. Read the sentences.
Mark the sentence that goes with the picture.

1

○ You have more than 200 bones.

○ You have less than 50 bones.

2

○ Bones are not alive.

○ Bones give you shape.

3

○ A joint lets you bend and move.

○ A joint keeps you safe.

4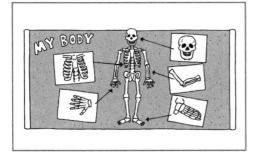

○ Bones need calcium.

○ Shapes need calcium.

I Use New Words

Write the missing word to complete the sentence.
Then read the sentence.

1 | safe   calcium |

Some foods have _____.

2 | bone   joint |

A _____ lets you bend.

3 | skeleton   change |

A _____ is made of bones.

4 | foods   parts |

Bones and joints are body _____.

5 | alive   work |

Bones are _____.

I Write About It

1 Draw a picture of how you would look if you did <u>not</u> have a skeleton.
Hint: Could you sit on a bike seat?

2 Could you ride a bike with no bones in your body? Write about it.

_____

_____

_____

3 Write a sentence to tell how you are using your joints now.

_____

_____

_____

My Skeletal System

Topic: My Skeletal System
Big Question: Can I live without my bones?

Tie It Together

Use the script below to guide students in discussing the Big Question and what they have learned about the topic from the paired texts. Feel free to expand on these questions and responses.

Questions	Sample Responses
Think about the books you read. What are some ways that your skeleton helps you live every day?	*My skeleton holds me up so I can sit on my bike and do other things. My skeleton protects other body parts, such as my brain and heart. Bones in my skeleton make new blood that my body needs to live.*
What happens if a bone gets broken?	*If a bone gets broken, a person needs to go to a doctor. The doctor will look at the bone and take an X-ray, or picture of the bone. Then the doctor might put a cast on it. The cast holds the bone in place while it gets better.*
Are bones alive?	*Yes, bones are alive. They grow and change. Most bones make new blood for your body.*
What is a joint?	*A joint is a part where your bones meet together. A joint lets you bend and move.*
Point to, and name, some places on your body where you have joints.	*Students may point to and name: knees, elbows, wrists, ankles, toes, knuckles, hips, etc.*
Both books mention some ways to take care of your bones. What are the ways?	*Eat healthy foods: vegetables, fruits, and foods that have calcium such as milk, almonds, cheese, and broccoli (other examples: yogurt, salmon, and leafy greens such as spinach or kale). It is also important to drink water and exercise.*
Our Big Question was "Can I live without my bones?" How did the book *Jacob's Arm* answer this question?	Jacob's Arm: *If I didn't have bones, I would not be able to ride a bike. Also, bones protect other parts that are inside of me if I fall down. So, I learned that I can't live without my bones.*
How did the book *How Bones Work* answer it?	How Bones Work: *Bones give me shape, hold me up, keep body parts safe, and make new blood. I would not be able to live without my bones.*

I Read and Understand

Read the sentence. Mark the best answer.

1 Your body has bones that make up a ____.

○ cast

○ bike

○ skeleton

2 Joints help you ____.

○ drink water

○ bend and move

○ eat food with calcium

3 ____ is good for your bones.

○ Healthy food

○ A big crash

○ A broken bike

4 Bones keep your ____ safe.

○ X-ray

○ move

○ body parts

I Can!

I can tell you about my skeleton and how I can take care of my bones.

1

Draw a picture of something that helps broken bones get better.	Draw a picture of something that is good for your bones.

2 What are some ways that your bones help you live? Write about them.

_____

_____

_____

_____

_____

_____

Earth's Moon and Sun

Student Objective:

Students will learn facts about the moon and the sun and will be able to describe differences between them.

Big Question:

Would you like to visit the moon or the sun?

Topic Introduction:

Explain to students that the moon and sun are both part of our solar system. Tell them that we can see the sun every day and the moon every night. Explain that scientists study the moon and the sun to help us learn more about them. Tell students that they will read two books in which they will learn facts about the moon and the sun.

Paired Texts:

Assessment Materials:

Lesson Plan

1. Prepare for the Lesson

Minibook: Reproduce the minibook pages. Cut them in half and staple them together in numerical order. Distribute one minibook to each student.

Dictionary and Activity Pages: Reproduce and distribute to each student one copy of the Dictionary page and the following activity pages: I Read Closely, I Use New Words, and I Write About It.

2. Introduce the Minibook

Tell students that they will read a book about the moon and the sun. Explain that they will find out if the moon and the sun are the same.

3. Learn New Vocabulary

Guide students through the Dictionary page. Read each word aloud as you point to the picture. Have students echo you. Point out the following:

- In this selection, the word *surface* means "the outside layer of the moon and sun."

For the Words to Know at the bottom of the page, read each word aloud and have students echo you. Point out the following:

- *Gases* are a type of matter that is not liquid or solid. Explain that *gases* float and that many gases burn easily.

- The letters *ar* in the words *far* and *star* have this sound: /ar/.

- The letters *igh* in the word *light* have the long i sound.

4. Read the Minibook

Lead students in a choral reading of the minibook. Then guide students in discussing what they have read. Help them identify the following:

- **Main idea**—Our moon and sun are both far away. The moon is made of rock, and the sun is a star made of hot gases.

- **Supporting details**—The moon has a solid surface and people have walked on it. The moon does not make its own light and heat. The sun makes its own light and heat. We can see the moon because the sun shines on it.

5. Read the Teacher's Complex Text

Read the Teacher's Complex Text (p. 39) as students look at the pictures in their minibooks. Before you begin reading, say:

Look at the pictures in your book as I read aloud more information about "Are the Moon and the Sun the Same?" Look at the picture on page 1. Listen as I read.

6. Complete the Activity Pages

Guide students through completing the I Read Closely, I Use New Words, and I Write About It activities. Have students use their minibooks to help them answer questions and find information.

Teacher's Complex Text

Minibook Page 1

Earth has a moon and a sun. We can see them in the sky. They are very far away. The moon is about 240,000 miles from Earth. The sun is about 93,000,000 miles from Earth.

Minibook Page 2

The moon and the sun are not the same. They are made of different things. The moon is made mostly of rock. The sun is a star made of hot gases. The sun's gases have a lot of energy to make light and heat.

Minibook Page 3

The moon and the sun are not the same. The moon has a solid surface with dry, dusty land and big ice patches. The sun does not have a solid surface. The sun's surface is very hot and has bubbly, fiery flares.

Minibook Page 4

The moon and the sun are not the same. The moon does not make light and heat. The sun makes its own light and heat. It is always very, very hot. On Earth, we can feel the heat from the sun.

Minibook Page 5

The moon and the sun are not the same. The sun shines on the moon. It shines on the part of the moon that we see. The part that we see changes on different nights. The moon looks like it changes shape.

Minibook Page 6

The moon and sun are not the same. Astronauts have walked on the moon. People can't go to the sun. It is so hot that no one can even get close to it.

Minibook Page 7

Now we know that the moon and sun are not the same in many ways!

	Very Far Away	Made of Rock	Made of Hot Gases	Makes Light	People Have Walked on It
moon	X	X			X
sun	X		X	X	

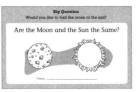

Minibook Title Page

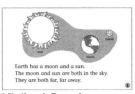

Minibook Page 1

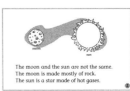

Minibook Page 2

Minibook Page 3

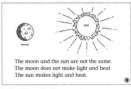

Minibook Page 4

Minibook Page 5

Minibook Page 6

Minibook Page 7

Dictionary

Read each word aloud.

Earth

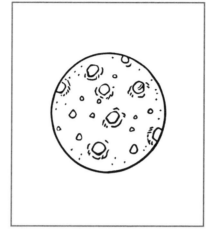

moon

rock

sky

sun

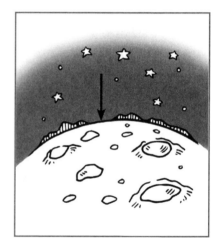

surface

Words to Know

far	gases	heat	light
mostly	near	people	same
shine	solid	star	walked

Are the Moon and the Sun the Same?

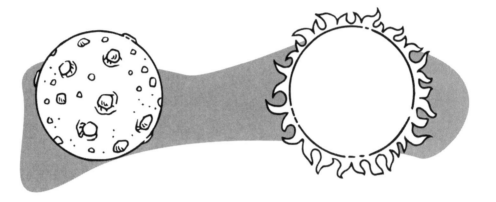

Name: _____

Earth has a moon and a sun.
The moon and sun are both in the sky.
They are both far, far away.

1

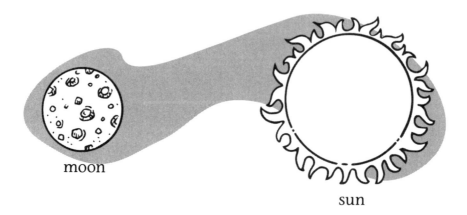

moon

sun

The moon and the sun are not the same.
The moon is made mostly of rock.
The sun is a star made of hot gases.

2

moon

sun

The moon and the sun are not the same.
The moon has a solid surface.
The sun does not have a solid surface.

3

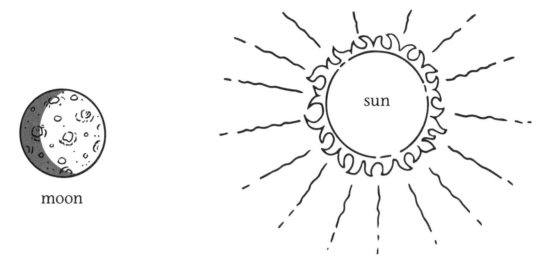

moon

sun

The moon and the sun are not the same.
The moon does not make light and heat.
The sun makes light and heat.

The moon and the sun are not the same.
The moon does not shine on the sun.
The sun shines on the moon.

The moon and sun are not the same.
People have walked on the moon.
People can't go near the sun.

6

Comparing the Moon and the Sun

	Very Far Away	Made of Rock	Made of Hot Gases	Makes Light	People Have Walked on It
moon	X	X			X
sun	X		X	X	

Now I know that the moon and the
sun are not the same!

7

I Read Closely

Look at the picture. Read the sentences.
Mark the sentence that goes with the picture.

1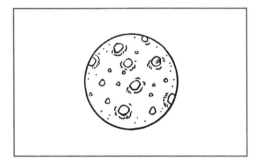

○ The moon is mostly rock.

○ The sun is mostly rock.

2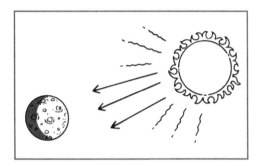

○ The sun shines on the moon.

○ The moon shines on the sun.

3

○ The moon is a star made of hot gases.

○ The sun is a star made of hot gases.

4

○ People can't go near the sun.

○ People have walked on the sun.

I Use New Words

Write the missing word to complete the sentence.
Then read the sentence.

1   rock   star

The sun is a _____.

2   same   gases

The moon and sun are not the _____.

3   sky   heat

I see the moon in the _____.

4   rock   sun

The _____ shines.

5   light   Earth

People can walk on _____.

I Write About It

1 Write a sentence that tells how the moon and the sun are not the same.

_____

_____

_____

2 Would you like to walk on the moon or the sun? Write about it.

_____

_____

_____

_____

_____

Draw a picture about what you wrote.

Lesson Plan

1. Prepare for the Lesson

Minibook: Reproduce the minibook pages. Cut them in half and staple them together in numerical order. Distribute one minibook to each student.

Dictionary and Activity Pages: Reproduce and distribute to each student one copy of the Dictionary page and the following activity pages: I Read Closely, I Use New Words, and I Write About It.

2. Introduce the Minibook

Tell students that they will read a book about the moon. Tell them that they will learn about what the moon is like and why it looks like it changes shape.

3. Learn New Vocabulary

Guide students through the Dictionary page. Read each word aloud as you point to the picture. Have students echo you. Point out the following:

- In this book, the word *craters* means "large round holes in the ground made by falling rocks."

- In this book, the word *space* means "the area beyond Earth where the stars and planets are."

For the Words to Know at the bottom of the page, read each word aloud and have students echo you. Point out the following:

- The word *breathe* means "to take air into and out of your lungs."

- The letters *igh* in the words *light* and *night* have the long i sound.

4. Read the Minibook

Lead students in a choral reading of the minibook. Then guide students in discussing what they have read. Help them identify the following:

- **Main idea**—The moon does not have people, plants, or animals. It moves around Earth about once every 29 days.

- **Supporting details**—The sun shines its light on the moon. The moon looks like it changes shape. It looks different every night.

5. Read the Teacher's Complex Text

Read the Teacher's Complex Text (p. 49) as students look at the pictures in their minibooks. Before you begin reading, say:

Look at the pictures in your book as I read aloud more information about "Earth's Moon." Look at the picture on page 1. Listen as I read.

6. Complete the Activity Pages

Guide students through completing the I Read Closely, I Use New Words, and I Write About It activities. Have students use their minibooks to help them answer questions and find information.

Teacher's Complex Text

Minibook Title Page

Minibook Page 1

The moon is our nearest neighbor in space. It is easy to see it at night. The moon is smaller than Earth. It is smaller than the sun, too.

Minibook Page 1

Minibook Page 2

The moon has no air. No people, plants, or animals live there. The moon has tall mountains and flat, dusty plains.

Minibook Page 2

Minibook Page 3

Astronauts have walked on the moon. They had to wear spacesuits and take air to breathe. The air came from a hose attached to the spacecraft or from a special backpack. They also had to take food and drinking water with them.

Minibook Page 3

Minibook Page 4

Many space rocks hit the moon's surface. The rocks make big holes, called craters. There is no air to protect the moon from space rocks. There is no wind to wear away the craters. Scientists have discovered that some of the craters have huge patches of ice.

Minibook Page 4

Minibook Page 5

The sun shines its light on the moon. The moon does not make light. We see the part of the moon that the sun shines on. If the sun weren't there, we wouldn't be able to see the moon at all.

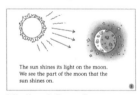

Minibook Page 5

Minibook Page 6

The moon orbits, or moves around, Earth about every 29 days. The part of the moon that we see changes. The part facing the sun is lit up. The part facing away from the sun stays dark.

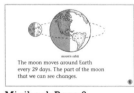

Minibook Page 6

Minibook Page 7

The moon looks like it changes shape. We are really seeing the moon lit up by the sun in different ways on different nights. We call these changing views of the moon, the moon phases. The moon looks different every night.

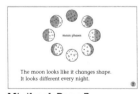

Minibook Page 7

Dictionary

Read each word aloud.

air

craters

Earth

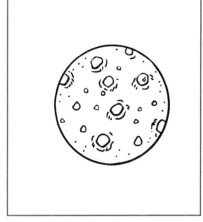

moon

space

sun

Words to Know

breathe	changes	different	light
live	night	part	shines
smaller	special	suits	wore

Earth's Moon

Name: _____

We can see the moon in space.
It is smaller than Earth.

1

The moon has no air.
No people, plants, or animals live there.

2

People have walked on the moon.
They wore special suits.
They took air to breathe.

3

Many space rocks hit the moon.
The rocks make big craters.

4

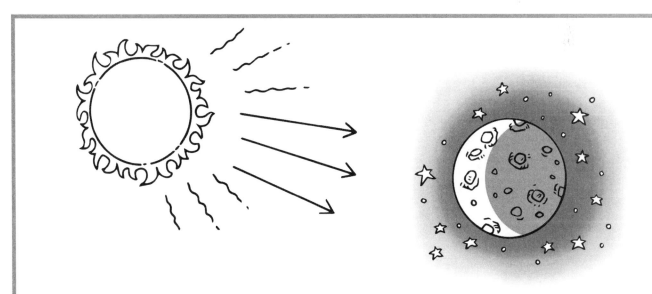

The sun shines its light on the moon.
We see the part of the moon that the
sun shines on.

5

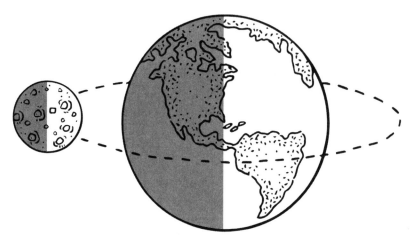

moon's orbit

The moon moves around Earth
every 29 days. The part of the moon
that we can see changes.

6

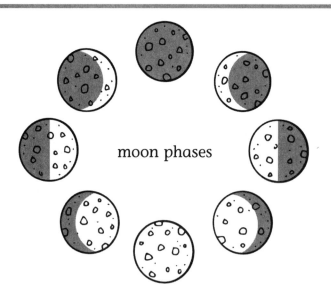

moon phases

The moon looks like it changes shape.
It looks different every night.

7

Name: _____

I Read Closely

Look at the picture. Read the sentences.
Mark the sentence that goes with the picture.

1

   ○ We cannot see the moon in space.

   ○ We can see the moon in space.

2

   ○ No people, plants, or animals live on the moon.

   ○ People, plants, and animals live on the moon.

3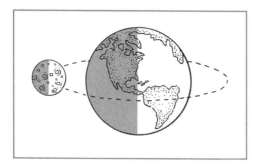

   ○ Earth moves around the moon every 29 days.

   ○ The moon moves around Earth every 29 days.

4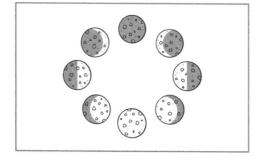

   ○ The moon changes shape.

   ○ The moon looks like it changes shape.

Name: _____

I Use New Words

Write the missing word to complete the sentence.
Then read the sentence.

1   light   crater

A big rock makes a _____ on the moon.

2   Earth   space

We live on _____.

3   shines   suits

The sun _____ on the moon.

4   air   animals

We need _____ to breathe.

5   wore   changes

The moon looks like it _____ shape.

I Write About It

Look at the picture. Answer the questions.

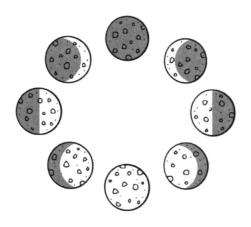

1 Does the moon really change shape?
Write a sentence to tell about it.

_____

_____

_____

_____

2 How does the moon get craters?
Write a sentence to tell about it.

_____

_____

_____

_____

Earth's Moon and Sun

Topic: Earth's Moon and Sun
Big Question: Would you like to visit the moon or the sun?

Tie It Together

Use the script below to guide students in discussing the Big Question and what they have learned about the topic from the paired texts. Feel free to expand on these questions and responses.

Questions	Sample Responses
Think about the books you read. What are some examples of how the moon and sun are different?	*The moon is made of rock. The sun is made of hot gases. The moon does not make light and heat. The sun makes light and heat. People have walked on the moon. People can't go near the sun.*
What are some ways that the moon and the sun are the same?	*They are both in space, and they are far, far away.*
How can we see the moon if it does not make light?	*We see the part of the moon that the sun is shining on. Since the moon is moving around Earth, the sun shines on different parts of the moon every night. That is why the moon looks different every night.*
Do animals, plants, or people live on the moon?	*The moon has no air. No animals, plants, or people live on the moon.*
What are some things that people had to take with them to walk on the moon?	*People who walked on the moon had to take air to breathe and special suits to wear.*
Neither book said that people have walked on the sun. Explain why.	*The sun does not have a solid surface like the moon. It is a star made of hot gases. People can't go near the sun because it is much too hot.*
Our Big Question was "Would you like to visit the moon or the sun?" How did the book Are the Moon and the Sun the Same? answer this question?	Answers will vary.
How did the book Earth's Moon answer it?	Answers will vary.

Name: _____

I Read and Understand

Read the sentence. Mark the best answer.

1 The moon is made mostly of ____.

○ rock

○ plants

○ gases

2 The ____ makes light and heat.

○ Earth

○ sun

○ moon

3 The sun does not have a solid ____.

○ crater

○ air

○ surface

4 People have walked on the ____.

○ star

○ moon

○ sun

I Can!

I can share facts about the moon and the sun.

1 Write three facts about the moon and the sun.

moon	sun
1. _____	1. _____
2. _____	2. _____
3. _____	3. _____

2 Would you like to visit the moon or the sun? Write about it.

_____

_____

_____

_____

_____

_____

_____

Everything Is Made of Matter

Student Objective: Students will understand that matter can be a solid, a liquid, or a gas.

Big Question: ## What is the same about water, a toy, and air?

Topic Introduction: Explain to students that everything is made of matter. Point out things around the classroom that are examples of solid, liquid, and gas. Tell students that they will read two books that will tell them about matter.

Paired Texts:

Assessment Materials:

Lesson Plan

1. Prepare for the Lesson

Minibook: Reproduce the minibook pages. Cut them in half and staple them together in numerical order. Distribute one minibook to each student.

Dictionary and Activity Pages: Reproduce and distribute to each student one copy of the Dictionary page and the following activity pages: I Read Closely, I Use New Words, and I Write About It.

2. Introduce the Minibook

Before the lesson, display a book, a glass of water, and an inflated balloon. Tell students that these objects show us the three forms of matter: solid, liquid, gas. Explain that everything around them, including air, is made up of matter. Tell students that they will read a book about the three forms of matter.

3. Learn New Vocabulary

Guide students through the Dictionary page. Read each word aloud as you point to the picture. Have students echo you. Point out the following:

- For the word *solid,* tell students that a book is an example of a solid object. Point out other solid objects around the room.

For the Words to Know at the bottom of the page, read each word aloud and have students echo you. Point out the following:

- In this book, *matter* means "anything that has weight and takes up space."

4. Read the Minibook

Lead students in a choral reading of the minibook. Then guide students in discussing what they have read. Help them identify the following:

- **Main idea**—Everything is matter. Matter has three forms: solid, liquid, and gas.

- **Supporting details**—A solid doesn't change its shape. A liquid can flow and takes the shape of its container. A gas is invisible and takes the shape of its container.

5. Read the Teacher's Complex Text

Read the Teacher's Complex Text (p. 63) as students look at the pictures in their minibooks. Before you begin reading, say:

Look at the pictures in your book as I read aloud more information about "What Is Matter?" Look at the picture on page 1. Listen as I read.

6. Complete the Activity Pages

Guide students through completing the I Read Closely, I Use New Words, and I Write About It activities. Have students use their minibooks to help them answer questions and find information.

Teacher's Complex Text

Minibook Page 1

Everything around us is made of matter. Think of a book, water, and air. It doesn't seem like these things have anything that is the same, but they do. They are all made up of matter. Matter is anything that takes up space. Matter has three forms: solid, liquid, and gas.

Minibook Page 2

Matter can be a solid. A solid object has a shape of its own. It is the easiest form of matter to see and feel. A book and a toy have a shape. They can be hard or soft. If I pick up a book or toy and place it somewhere else, it will stay the same shape, size, and weight.

Minibook Page 3

Matter can be a liquid. A liquid has no shape of its own. If I accidentally tip over a pail of water, the water will spill and flow all over the floor. The same would happen with other liquids, such as milk or juice. A liquid will take the shape of its container. A liquid will flow if it is not in a container.

Minibook Page 4

Matter can be a gas. A gas has no shape of its own. Air that you breathe is a gas. If air is in a balloon, it takes the shape of the balloon. A gas can be invisible. Even if you can't see it, it's there. Steam is also a gas. You can see steam floating from a teakettle.

Minibook Page 5

A solid keeps its shape. A book and a toy are examples of solids. A liquid can flow. Water and juice are examples of liquids. A gas can float. Air and steam are examples of gases.

Minibook Page 6

A book, water, and air all have different forms. They are solid, liquid, and gas. All of these things are made up of matter.

Minibook Page 7

Everything around us is solid, liquid, or gas. Everything is made of matter.

Minibook Title Page

Minibook Page 1

Minibook Page 2

Minibook Page 3

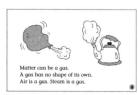

Minibook Page 4

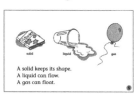

Minibook Page 5

Minibook Page 6

Minibook Page 7

Dictionary

Read each word aloud.

air

float

flow

gas

liquid

solid

Words to Know

everything	juice	matter	own
shape	steam	toy	water

What Is Matter?

Name: _____

Everything around us is made of matter.
Matter can be solid, liquid, or gas.

1

Matter can be a solid.
A solid has a shape of its own.
A book is a solid. A toy is a solid.

2

Matter can be a liquid.
A liquid has no shape of its own.
Water is a liquid. Juice is a liquid.

3

Matter can be a gas.
A gas has no shape of its own.
Air is a gas. Steam is a gas.

4

solid   liquid   gas

A solid keeps its shape.
A liquid can flow.
A gas can float.

5

All of these things are matter.

6

Everything is made of matter.
Matter is all around us.

7

Name: _____

I Read Closely

Look at the picture. Read the sentences.
Mark the sentence that goes with the picture.

1

○ A solid has a shape.

○ A liquid has a shape.

2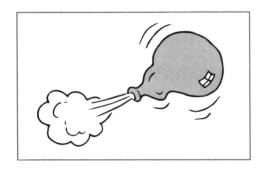

○ Air is a gas.

○ Juice is a gas.

3

○ A solid can flow.

○ A liquid can flow.

4

○ Everything is made of matter.

○ Everything is a solid.

I Use New Words

Write the missing word to complete the sentence.
Then read the sentence.

1

air   toys

My _____ are solids.

2

flow   solid

Water can _____.

3

water   matter

Everything is made of _____.

4

solid   shape

Juice has no _____.

5

liquid   gas

Air is a _____.

Name: _____

I Write About It

1   Look at the picture. Write **S** on something that is a solid.
Write **L** on something that is a liquid. Then write **G** on
something that is a gas.

2   Look around you. Write a sentence about something you see
for each form of matter.

solid

_____

_____

liquid

_____

_____

gas

_____

_____

Lesson Plan

1. Prepare for the Lesson

Minibook: Reproduce the minibook pages. Cut them in half and staple them together in numerical order. Distribute one minibook to each student.

Dictionary and Activity Pages: Reproduce and distribute to each student one copy of the Dictionary page and the following activity pages: I Read Closely, I Use New Words, and I Write About It.

2. Introduce the Minibook

Tell students they will read a book about water and how it can be solid, liquid, or gas, depending on its temperature.

3. Learn New Vocabulary

Guide students through the Dictionary page. Read each word aloud as you point to the picture. Have students echo you. Point out the following:

- The words *drip, float, flow, melt,* and *splash* tell what water can do.

For the Words to Know at the bottom of the page, read each word aloud and have students echo you. Point out the following:

- The word *freeze* means "to become solid or icy at a very cold temperature."

- In this book, the word *gas* means "an invisible substance that you can't see." For example, the air you breathe is a gas.

- The word *steam* means "the gas that hot water makes."

4. Read the Minibook

Lead students in a choral reading of the minibook. Then guide students in discussing what they have read. Help them identify the following:

- **Main idea**—Water can be solid, liquid, or gas.

- **Supporting details**—Cold or hot temperatures can make water change its form.

5. Read the Teacher's Complex Text

Read the Teacher's Complex Text (p. 73) as students look at the pictures in their minibooks. Before you begin reading, say:

Look at the pictures in your book as I read aloud more information about "Wonderful Water." Look at the picture on page 1. Listen as I read.

6. Complete the Activity Pages

Guide students through completing the I Read Closely, I Use New Words, and I Write About It activities. Have students use their minibooks to help them answer questions and find information.

Teacher's Complex Text

Minibook Title Page

Minibook Page 1
Think about places where you have seen water. You have probably seen water flowing out of a hose. You may have also seen ice and steam. Is water solid, liquid, or gas?

Minibook Page 1

Minibook Page 2
It can be all three! Water changes as its temperature changes. Water can get very hot, very cold, or it can be a temperature in between. Water can change. Water can be all three forms of matter. It can be solid, liquid, or gas!

Minibook Page 2

Minibook Page 3
Water can be a liquid. You can see water falling as rain or flowing down a river. Liquid water is probably the way we see it the most each day. You can pour water into a glass. Water takes the shape of the glass. Water can flow, splash, and drip.

Minibook Page 3

Minibook Page 4
Water can be a gas. Heat turns water into a gas called steam. When water gets very hot, it turns into steam. You can see steam floating from water that is heated in a teakettle. You can also see steam floating when you take a hot shower.

Minibook Page 4

Minibook Page 5
Water can be a solid. When water freezes, it turns into a solid. Solid water is ice or snow. Solid water can be thick like a frozen pond you can skate on, or it can be thin, like a tiny, delicate snowflake. Solid water can also be ice from your freezer.

Minibook Page 5

Minibook Page 6
Solid water can change back into liquid water. When ice warms up, it melts. Heat changes ice, or solid water, back into liquid water.

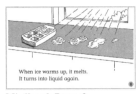

Minibook Page 6

Minibook Page 7
Water is wonderful. If the temperature of water gets very cold, very hot, or in between, water can change. It can be solid, liquid, or gas.

Minibook Page 7

Name: _____

Dictionary

Read each word aloud.

drip

floats

flow

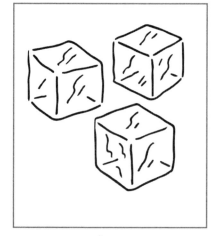

ice

melts

splash

freezes	gas	liquid	solid
steam	think	turns	warms
water	wonderful		

Big Question

What is the same about water, a toy, and air?

Wonderful Water

Name: _____

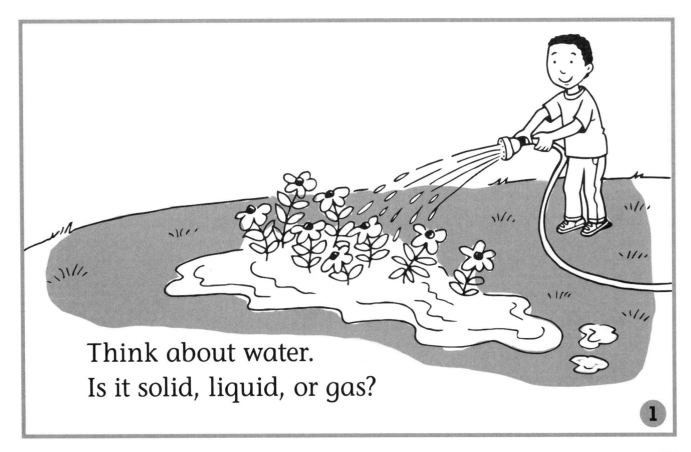

Think about water.
Is it solid, liquid, or gas?

1

It can be all three!
Water is wonderful!

2

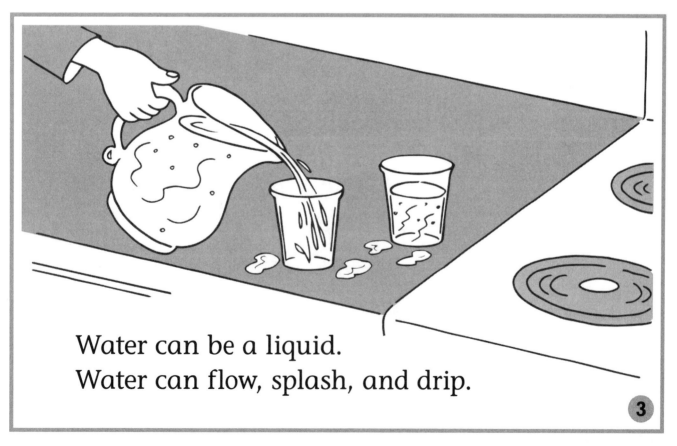

Water can be a liquid.
Water can flow, splash, and drip.

3

    Reading Paired Text • EMC 1371 • © Evan-Moor Corp.

Water can be a gas.
The gas is called steam.
Steam floats.

4

Water can be a solid.
When water freezes, it turns into a solid.
Solid water is ice.

5

When ice warms up, it melts.
It turns into liquid again.

6

Water is wonderful.
It can be solid, liquid, or gas.

7

Name: _____

I Read Closely

Look at the picture. Read the sentences.
Mark the sentence that goes with the picture.

1

○ Solid water is gas.

○ Solid water is ice.

2

○ Heat will make ice melt to
   a liquid.

○ Heat will make water change
   to a solid.

3

○ Liquid water is steam.

○ Liquid water can flow.

4

○ If ice warms up, it melts.

○ If ice warms up, it freezes.

I Use New Words

Write the missing word to complete the sentence.
Then read the sentence.

1   glass   think

I can put water in a _____.

2   heat   gas

Steam is a _____.

3   solid   liquid

Water that freezes turns into a _____.

4   freeze   flow

If you spill water, it will _____.

5   melt   splash

Ice will _____ in the sun.

I Write About It

1 Draw pictures of water as solid, liquid, and gas. Label each picture.

2 How can you make water change from a solid to a liquid? Write about it.

_____

_____

_____

3 How can you make water change from a liquid to a gas? Write about it.

_____

_____

_____

Everything Is Made of Matter

Topic: Everything Is Made of Matter

Big Question: What is the same about water, a toy, and air?

Tie It Together

Use the script below to guide students in discussing the Big Question and what they have learned about the topic from the paired texts. Feel free to expand on these questions and responses.

Questions	Sample Responses
Think about the books you read. You learned that everything is made of matter. What are the three forms of matter?	*The three forms of matter are solid, liquid, and gas.*
What are some things that are solids?	*Toys, ice, and books are examples of solids.*
What are some things that are liquids?	*Water and juice are examples of liquids.*
What are some things that are gases?	*Air and steam are examples of gases.*
Explain how water can change from a liquid to a solid.	*Water is a liquid. When it freezes, it turns into a solid. Ice is an example of water that turned into a solid.*
Explain how water can change from a liquid to a gas.	*If water is heated, it creates steam. Steam is a gas. You can see steam when water is heated in a teakettle.*
Our Big Question was "What is the same about water, a toy, and air?" How did the book *What Is Matter?* answer this question?	What Is Matter?: *Everything around us is made of matter. So we know that water, a toy, and air are all different forms of matter.*
How did the book *Wonderful Water* answer it?	Wonderful Water: *Water is matter and so are a toy and air. They are the same because they are all made of matter.*

I Read and Understand

Read the sentence. Mark the best answer.

1 The forms of matter are ____.

○ solid, big, liquid

○ solid, liquid, gas

○ liquid, gas, hot

2 Ice, toys, and books are ____.

○ solids

○ liquids

○ gases

3 Steam is water that changed to a ____.

○ gas

○ liquid

○ matter

4 Everything around us is made of ____.

○ gas

○ solids

○ matter

Name: _____

I Can!

I can tell you about the three forms of matter.

1 Draw something to show each form of matter.

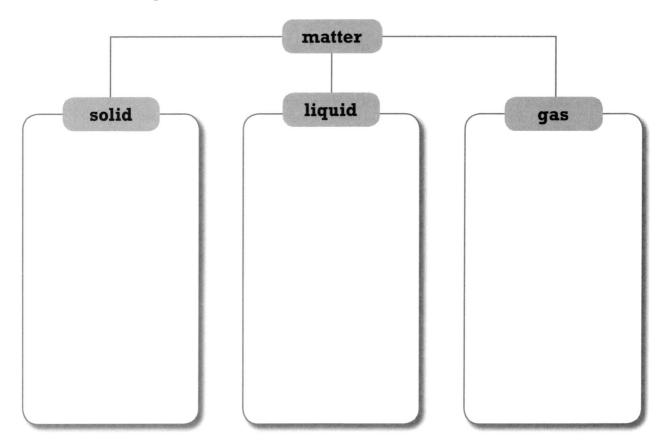

2 What is the same about water, a toy, and air?
Write a sentence that tells about it.

_____

_____

_____

_____

Animal Classification

Student Objective: Students will understand that herbivores, carnivores, and omnivores have different kinds of teeth that are designed to help them eat different foods.

Big Question:

Why do animals have different kinds of teeth?

Topic Introduction: Explain to students that animals have the kinds of teeth they need to eat the food that is just right for them. Tell students that they will read two selections that will tell about animals, the kinds of teeth they have, and the types of food they eat.

Paired Text Selections:

Assessment Materials:

Lesson Plan

1. Prepare for the Lesson

Reproduce and distribute to each student one copy of the selection, the Dictionary page, and the following activity pages: I Read Closely, I Use New Words, and I Write About It.

2. Introduce the Selection

Before the lesson, find a picture of a domestic (farm) goat and display it where students can see it. Explain to students that there are many different kinds of goats. Some goats are wild, but many are raised on farms or as pets. Tell them that in this selection, they will read a poem about goats and how they eat.

3. Learn New Vocabulary

Guide students through the Dictionary page. Read each word aloud as you point to the picture. Have students echo you. Point out the following:

- In this selection, the word *herd* means "a group of animals of the same kind."

For the Words to Know at the bottom of the page, read each word aloud and have students echo you. Point out the following:

- In this selection, the word *bark* means "the covering on a tree."

- The word *crunch* means "to chew noisily."

- The word *grind* means "to crush."

4. Read the Selection

Lead students in a choral reading of the selection. Then guide students in discussing what they have read. Help them identify the following:

- **Main idea**—Goats are plant eaters that eat mostly grass.

- **Supporting details**—Goats have teeth that are flat on top and are perfect for grinding grass and plants.

5. Read the Teacher's Complex Text

Read the Teacher's Complex Text (p. 87) as students look at the pictures in their selection. Before you begin reading, say:

Look at the pictures in your selection as I read aloud more information about "Goats." Look at the first picture on page 89. Listen as I read.

6. Complete the Activity Pages

Guide students through completing the I Read Closely, I Use New Words, and I Write About It activities. Have students use their selections to help them answer questions and find information.

Teacher's Complex Text

Goats are very smart, curious animals. They are herbivores, or plant eaters. They like to graze and eat fresh, green grass and plants that grow in fields and on hillsides. Goats have very good balance. They can walk on steep hillsides and some places that are too dangerous for people. Some goats even climb trees to find food!

Goats will nibble on things like tree bark and roses. Fresh grass is the healthiest food for them, so that is what they need to eat the most. Goats know how to pick out and eat the most nutritious parts of plants.

Goats' teeth are made to chew and grind grasses and plants. Adult goats have no top middle teeth. They have a full set of flat-topped teeth on the bottom. They keep chewing until the grass and plants are in small enough bits to swallow. A goat's back teeth fit together very tightly. You do not want to put your finger in the back of a goat's mouth!

In places that have problems with fires, such as California and Arizona, goats can help get rid of tall weeds and brush. Goat herds graze where it is too steep for people to go. Grazing helps, because there is less grass to catch on fire. A herd of goats can clear land much faster than a crew of people. So, if you need some mowing done, a small herd of goats can do the mowing for you!

A baby goat is called a kid. Look at the chart. It shows how a kid goat's teeth grow and change. A kid goat's teeth grow bigger as it gets older. It's teeth are flat on top. Flat teeth are good for grinding grass, roses, and other plants.

student selection, pg. 89

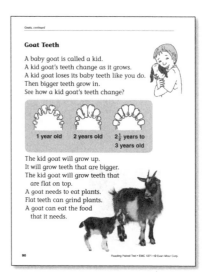

student selection, pg. 90

Dictionary

Read each word aloud.

chew

goats

herd

mow

roses

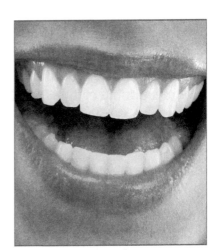
teeth

Words to Know

bark	because	change	clue
crunch	eaters	flat	grind
meat	think	tummy	yummy

Goats

Goats are plant eaters,
No meat will do.
Goats want grass to crunch
And plants to chew.

Goats think trees and bark
Are really yummy.
Some roses and grass
Are good for a goat's tummy.

A goat's teeth can grind,
Because they are flat on top.
Goats chew side to side
Until they are ready to stop.

If you need to mow,
I give you this clue.
A small herd of goats
Can mow for you.

Goat Teeth

A baby goat is called a kid.
A kid goat's teeth change as it grows.
A kid goat loses its baby teeth like you do.
Then bigger teeth grow in.
See how a kid goat's teeth change?

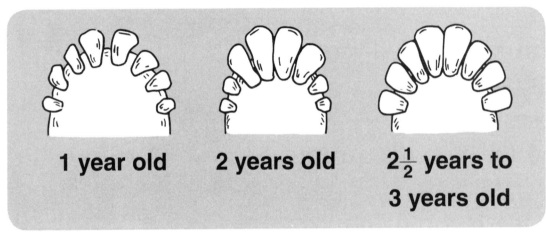

1 year old **2 years old** **$2\frac{1}{2}$ years to 3 years old**

The kid goat will grow up.
It will grow teeth that are bigger.
The kid goat will grow teeth that
    are flat on top.
A goat needs to eat plants.
Flat teeth can grind plants.
A goat can eat the food
    that it needs.

Name: _____

I Read Closely

Look at the picture. Read the sentences.
Mark the sentence that goes with the picture.

1

○ Goats like to eat meat.

○ Goats like to eat plants.

2

○ Some roses and grass are good for a goat's tummy.

○ Trees and bark are good for a goat's tummy.

3

○ Goat teeth are funny.

○ Goat teeth are flat.

4

○ Goats can help mow.

○ Goats can give you a clue.

I Use New Words

Write the missing word to complete the sentence.
Then read the sentence.

1 | clue   crunch |

A _____ helps you find out.

2 | think   mow |

To cut the grass is to _____.

3 | grind   herd |

A lot of goats is a _____.

4 | yummy   tummy |

A food you like to eat is _____.

5 | meat   chew |

I _____ my food when I eat.

I Write About It

1 Draw a picture of a food that is good for goats to eat.
Then write about it.

_____

_____

_____

_____

_____

_____

2 What is something that goats can do for you?
Write about it.

_____

_____

_____

_____

Word Bank

crunch   eat   grind   mow   plants

Lesson Plan

1. Prepare for the Lesson

Reproduce and distribute to each student one copy of the selection, the Dictionary page, and the following activity pages: I Read Closely, I Use New Words, and I Write About It.

2. Introduce the Selection

Tell students that in this selection, they will read about three different groups of animals that can be sorted by the type of teeth they have and the kinds of food they eat in the wild.

3. Learn New Vocabulary

Guide students through the Dictionary page. Read each word aloud as you point to the picture. Have students echo you. Point out the following:

- *Bite* (cut) and *grind* (crush) describe actions of teeth chewing when animals eat.

For the Words to Know at the bottom of the page, read each word aloud and have students echo you. Point out the following:

- In this selection, *wild* animals are animals that live in nature.

- Students will learn about three different groups of animals called *herbivores* (plant eaters), *carnivores* (meat eaters), and *omnivores* (plant and meat eaters).

4. Read the Selection

Begin by helping students identify the animals pictured in the selection. Point to each label as you read it aloud. Then lead students in a choral reading of the selection. After you read, guide students in discussing what they have read. Help them identify the following:

- **Main idea**—Many animals can be grouped by the types of teeth they have and by the kinds of food they eat.

- **Supporting details**—Herbivores have flat teeth and eat plants, carnivores have pointed teeth and eat meat, and omnivores have flat and pointed teeth and eat both plants and meat.

5. Read the Teacher's Complex Text

Read the Teacher's Complex Text (p. 95) as students look at the pictures in their selection. Before you begin reading, say:

Look at the pictures in your selection as I read aloud more information about "Wild About Food." Look at the first picture on page 97. Listen as I read.

6. Complete the Activity Pages

Guide students through completing the I Read Closely, I Use New Words, and I Write About It activities. Have students use their selections to help them answer questions and find information.

Teacher's Complex Text

How are a rabbit and a deer the same? They both eat plants. Animals that eat only plants are called herbivores. Moose, deer, sheep, and rabbits are examples of herbivores. Herbivores have teeth that are flat on top, so they can chew and grind plants. Many herbivores graze and eat all day to have the energy they need.

How are a tiger and a wolf the same? They both eat meat. Animals that eat other animals are called carnivores. Lions, wolves, bears, and tigers are examples of carnivores. Carnivore teeth are sharp and pointed, so they can bite and tear meat. Carnivores get a lot of exercise because they have to hunt for the animals they eat. Carnivores help nature keep a balance so that there are not too many of one kind of animal.

How are a bear and a raccoon the same? They both eat plants and animals. Animals that eat plants and other animals are called omnivores. Raccoons, bears, pigs, and rats are omnivores. Omnivores eat mostly flowering plants. Some omnivores hunt for their meat, and others eat dead animals. Many omnivores eat animal eggs. Some omnivores eat insects. Omnivores have some teeth that are flat for grinding and some that are pointed for tearing meat.

Animals in the wild usually eat the kind of food that is best for them. Sometimes if they can't find enough of the right kind of food, then they might start eating other foods that are easy to find.

student selection, pg. 97

student selection, pg. 98

Dictionary

Read each word aloud.

bite

chew

eggs

flat

pointed

teeth

Words to Know

animals	called	carnivore	grind
herbivore	hunt	long	meat
omnivore	same	sharp	wild

Wild About Food

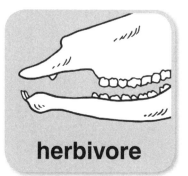

herbivore

How are a rabbit and a deer the same?
They both eat plants.
Animals that eat plants are called
    herbivores.
Herbivores have flat teeth.
They can chew and grind plants.
Plants are good for herbivores.
Herbivores eat all day long.

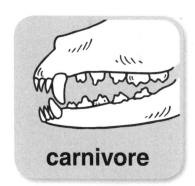

carnivore

How are a tiger and a wolf the same?
They both eat meat.
Animals that eat other animals are
    called carnivores.
Carnivores have sharp, pointed teeth.
They need to bite meat.
Meat is good for carnivores.
They hunt and eat a lot.

How are a bear and a raccoon the same?
They both eat plants and animals.
They have two kinds of teeth.
They have sharp and flat teeth.
Omnivores bite and chew meat.
They grind plants, too.
Some omnivores eat eggs or bugs.
Plants and animals are good
    for omnivores.

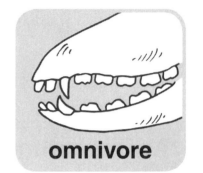

omnivore

Animals in the wild eat the kind
    of food that is good for them.

Name: _____

I Read Closely

Look at the picture. Read the sentences.
Mark the sentence that goes with the picture.

1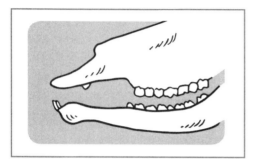

○ A herbivore has flat teeth.

○ A herbivore has sharp teeth.

2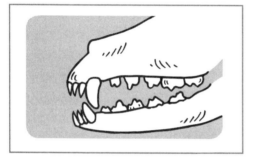

○ A carnivore has flat and sharp teeth.

○ A carnivore has only sharp teeth.

3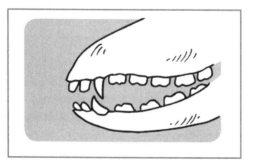

○ An omnivore has only flat teeth.

○ An omnivore has flat and sharp teeth.

4

○ I am an omnivore.

○ I am a herbivore.

Name: _____

I Use New Words

Write the missing word to complete the sentence.
Then read the sentence.

1   teeth   eggs

The bird sat on three _____.

2   Herbivores   Carnivores

_____ eat plants.

3   hunt   flat

Some animals _____ for food.

4   grind   bite

Pointed teeth can _____.

5   Omnivores   Herbivores

_____ eat meat and plants.

Name: _____

I Write About It

1 Use the words in the word bank to complete each sentence.

Word Bank

meat   plants   meat and plants

A raccoon likes to eat _____.

A deer likes to eat _____.

A wolf likes to eat _____.

2 Can a raccoon and a deer eat the same kind of food?
Write about it.

_____

_____

_____

_____

_____

Animal Classification

Topic: Animal Classification
Big Question: Why do animals have different kinds of teeth?

Tie It Together

Use the script below to guide students in discussing the Big Question and what they have learned about the topic from the paired selections. Feel free to expand on these questions and responses.

Questions	Sample Responses
Think about the selections you read. Which one is a poem, and how can you tell?	Goats *is a poem. It has short lines and rhyming words. It has a rhythm when I read it aloud.* Wild About Food *is not a poem. It has sentences and paragraphs. It does not have rhyming words. It does not have rhythm like a poem when I read it aloud.*
What kind of teeth do herbivores have?	*Herbivores have teeth that are flat on top. Herbivore teeth are good for grinding and chewing plants.*
What kind of teeth do carnivores have?	*Carnivores have teeth that are sharp and pointed. Carnivore teeth are good for biting and tearing meat.*
What kind of teeth do omnivores have?	*Omnivores have some flat teeth and some pointed teeth. Omnivore teeth can bite and tear meat. They can also grind and chew plants.*
The two selections compare some animals' teeth and what the animals eat. Explain how a goat and a deer are the same.	*A goat and a deer are both herbivores. They both eat plants. They both have flat teeth.*
Explain how a goat and a wolf are different.	*A goat is a herbivore (eats plants), and a wolf is a carnivore (eats meat).*
Our Big Question was "Why do animals have different kinds of teeth?" How did *Goats* answer this question?	Goats: *Goats need to eat plants, because that is the kind of food that is good for their bodies. They need teeth that are good for grinding and chewing plants. That's why they have teeth that are flat on top.*
How did *Wild About Food* answer it?	Wild About Food: *Different animals need different kinds of food to be healthy. Animals have the kind of teeth needed to eat the type of food that is good for them.*

I Read and Understand

Read the sentence. Mark the best answer.

1 Goats and deer like to eat ____.

○ bugs

○ plants

○ meat

2 A carnivore has teeth that are ____.

○ pointed

○ flat

○ soft

3 An omnivore has ____ teeth.

○ all flat

○ all pointed

○ flat and pointed

4 *Goats* and *Wild About Food* are mostly about ____.

○ animal teeth and food

○ an animal herd

○ how animals hunt

I Can!

I can tell about the teeth of herbivores, carnivores, and omnivores. I can tell about what they eat.

1 Draw a picture of each kind of teeth.

herbivore	carnivore	omnivore

2 Write a sentence that tells why a bear needs sharp and flat teeth.

_____

_____

_____

3 Write a sentence that tells why a tiger can't mow grass for you.

_____

_____

_____

Unit Overview
American Songs and Symbols

Student Objective: Students will learn the history of the traditional song *My Country 'Tis of Thee* and the history of a symbol of our country, the American flag.

Big Question:
What songs and symbols tell me I'm in America?

Topic Introduction: Explain to students that America has many traditions and symbols. Tell students that a tradition can be a celebration such as the Fourth of July or the singing of a song such as *My Country 'Tis of Thee*. Explain that some examples of American symbols are statues, flags, or buildings. For example, the White House is an American symbol. Then tell students that they will read a book about an American song and a book about an American symbol.

Paired Texts:

Assessment Materials:

Lesson Plan

1. Prepare for the Lesson

Minibook: Reproduce the minibook pages. Cut them in half and staple them together in numerical order. Distribute one minibook to each student.

Dictionary and Activity Pages: Reproduce and distribute to each student one copy of the Dictionary page and the following activity pages: I Read Closely, I Use New Words, and I Write About It.

2. Introduce the Minibook

Tell students that they will read a book about the traditional American song *My Country 'Tis of Thee.* Explain that they will learn what the words mean and why we sing the song.

3. Learn New Vocabulary

Guide students through the Dictionary page. Read each word aloud as you point to the picture. Have students echo you. Point out the following:

- *America* is another name for the United States.

- The *Liberty Bell* and the *Statue of Liberty* are American symbols.

- In this book, people who have come to live in America are called *pilgrims.*

For the Words to Know at the bottom of the page, read each word aloud and have students echo you. Point out the following:

- The word *ancestors* means "all the people who lived before us."

- The word *freedom* means "being allowed to do what you want."

4. Read the Minibook

Lead students in a choral reading of the minibook. Then guide students in discussing what they have read. Help them identify the following:

- **Main idea**—We are showing appreciation for our country and all the choices we can make about how we want to live.

- **Supporting details**—We appreciate the people who lived before us, and the beautiful land we enjoy. We have symbols such as the American flag, the Liberty Bell, and the Statue of Liberty.

5. Read the Teacher's Complex Text

Read the Teacher's Complex Text (p. 107) as students look at the pictures in their minibooks. Before you begin reading, say:

Look at the pictures in your book as I read more information about "My Country 'Tis of Thee." Look at the picture on page 1. Listen as I read.

6. Complete the Activity Pages

Guide students through completing the I Read Closely, I Use New Words, and I Write About It activities. Have students use their minibooks to help them answer questions and find information.

Teacher's Complex Text

Minibook Title Page

Minibook Page 1

My Country 'Tis of Thee is a song that celebrates, and says "thank you" for, the way that we all live together in a free country.

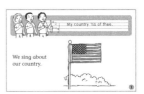

Minibook Page 1

Minibook Page 2

We sing about freedom and liberty. Having freedom means that we enjoy things like going to school, choosing the kind of job we want to do, deciding if we want to go to church, and making other decisions about how we live.

Minibook Page 2

Minibook Page 3

We sing about America. America is another name for the United States. We are singing to show appreciation for the land and everyone living in America.

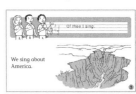

Minibook Page 3

Minibook Page 4

We sing about our ancestors. They are all the people who lived before us. Their bravery and hard work made it possible for us to live in a country where we can be free, be equal, work together, and have many choices.

Minibook Page 4

Minibook Page 5

We sing to say "thank you" to all the pilgrims who came to America. The Statue of Liberty is a symbol of welcome to people who come to this country. People came for many different reasons. Some wanted freedom and opportunity.

Minibook Page 5

Minibook Page 6

We sing about our beautiful land. We have tall mountains, green forests, lakes, and grassy plains. We can visit places to enjoy nature. Thank you to those who were here first, who had to share the land with so many new people.

Minibook Page 6

Minibook Page 7

We sing about the Liberty Bell. It was made as a symbol of freedom for America. It was built when the first Americans wanted to celebrate choosing their own leaders and making their own laws. Later, the bell became a symbol for people who wanted to stop slavery. It was rung to celebrate many important events in America.

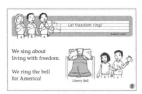

Minibook Page 7

Dictionary

Read each word aloud.

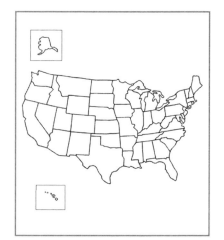

America

country

Liberty Bell

pilgrims

ring

Statue of Liberty

Words to Know

about	ancestors	beautiful	freedom
land	living	people	sing

My Country 'Tis of Thee

Name: _____

My country 'tis of thee,

We sing about
our country.

1

Sweet land of liberty,

We sing about
our freedom.

2

Of thee I sing;

We sing about
America.

3

Land where my fathers died,

We sing about our ancestors.

4

Land of the pilgrims' pride,

We sing about all the people who came to America.

Statue of Liberty

5

From every mountainside,

We sing about
our beautiful land.

6

Let freedom ring!

Samuel F. Smith

We sing about
living with freedom.

We ring the bell
for America!

Liberty Bell

7

I Read Closely

Look at the picture. Read the sentences.
Mark the sentence that goes with the picture.

1

  ○ We sing about our ancestors.

  ○ We sing about the land.

2

  ○ We sing about the bell.

  ○ We sing about our freedom.

3

  ○ We sing about the land.

  ○ We sing about people.

4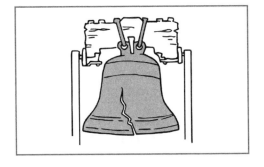

  ○ We sing about our country.

  ○ We ring the bell for America.

I Use New Words

Write the missing word to complete the sentence.
Then read the sentence.

1 freedom   living

"Liberty" means _____.

2 ring   sing

We can _____ about our country.

3 Statue of Liberty   America

The Liberty Bell is a symbol for _____.

4 ancestors   country

We are living after our _____.

5 land   pilgrims

The _____ went to a new country to live.

I Write About It

1 Draw a picture of something that you like to do in America.
Then write about it.

2 Draw a picture of something that will make America better for people.
Then write about it.

Lesson Plan

1. Prepare for the Lesson

Minibook: Reproduce the minibook pages. Cut them in half and staple them together in numerical order. Distribute one minibook to each student.

Dictionary and Activity Pages: Reproduce and distribute to each student one copy of the Dictionary page and the following activity pages: I Read Closely, I Use New Words, and I Write About It.

2. Introduce the Minibook

Before the lesson, display an American flag. Explain to students that it is a symbol of the United States. Tell students that they will read a book about our first official American flag and that they will learn how it changed to become the American flag we have today.

3. Learn New Vocabulary

Guide students through the Dictionary page. Read each word aloud as you point to the picture. Have students echo you. Point out the following:

- *America* is another name for the United States.

- The *colonies* were areas where groups of people from Europe settled after they arrived in America.

For the Words to Know at the bottom of the page, read each word aloud and have students echo you. Point out the following:

- The word *state* means "one of the 50 states in America."

4. Read the Minibook

Lead students in a choral reading of the minibook. Then guide students in discussing what they have read. Help them identify the following:

- **Main idea**—The first official stars and stripes flag was planned and approved by George Washington and some other leaders.

- **Supporting details**—Betsy Ross sewed the first flag in 1776. A new star was added with each new state, but the flag has kept 13 stripes for the original 13 colonies.

5. Read the Teacher's Complex Text

Read the Teacher's Complex Text (p. 117) as students look at the pictures in their minibooks. Before you begin reading, say:

Look at the pictures in your book as I read more information about "A Flag for America." Look at the picture on page 1. Listen as I read.

6. Complete the Activity Pages

Guide students through completing the I Read Closely, I Use New Words, and I Write About It activities. Have students use their minibooks to help them answer questions and find information.

Teacher's Complex Text

Minibook Title Page

Minibook Page 1

Long ago, when people first came to America, they lived in colonies. They had to follow the rules and laws of England. Some colonies had flags. A national flag for the 13 colonies was sometimes used, but it had a symbol for England on it.

Minibook Page 1

Minibook Page 2

During this time, America was trying to become free from England. The colonies wanted to make their own rules and laws. The colonists picked some leaders to be in a group called the Continental Congress. George Washington was part of that group. The leaders started planning a new flag.

Minibook Page 2

Minibook Page 3

One story says that George Washington asked his friend Betsy Ross, who was a seamstress, to make the first flag. She had a small shop where she sewed clothes, furniture, and flags. George Washington asked Betsy Ross to make the new stars and stripes flag. Betsy Ross finished making the new flag in June, 1776.

Minibook Page 3

Minibook Page 4

In 1777, the Continental Congress had a meeting. By this time, America was free from England. The leaders liked the new flag. They voted and passed a resolution (a promise) called the Flag Act to make the new stars and stripes flag the official flag for all the colonies.

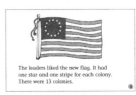

Minibook Page 4

Minibook Page 5

More and more people came to America. People moved west and settled in new areas. America grew and new states were added. For each new state, the flag got another star.

Minibook Page 5

Minibook Page 6

Now America has 50 states. The 50 stars on the flag stand for the 50 states. At first, leaders tried adding a new stripe for each state, but there wasn't room! The flag keeps 13 stripes to honor the original 13 colonies.

Minibook Page 6

Minibook Page 7

We see the American flag on government buildings and at other important places. It is pictured on the back of some of our paper money. The flag is a symbol of the hard work and cooperation of people long ago and today. It is a symbol for America.

Minibook Page 7

Dictionary

Read each word aloud.

America

Betsy Ross

colonies

George
Washington

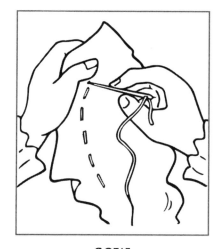
sew

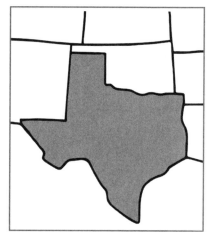
state

Words to Know

asked	flag	leaders	lived
more	people	places	star
stripe	symbol		

Big Question

What songs and symbols tell me I'm in America?

A Flag for America

Name: _____

Long ago, people came to America.
They lived in colonies.
Some colonies had flags.

The colonies had leaders.
One of them was George Washington.
They wanted a new flag.

2

In 1776, George Washington asked
Betsy Ross to sew the new flag.

3

The leaders liked the new flag. It had
one star and one stripe for each colony.
There were 13 colonies.

4

More people came to America.
The colonies became states.
The flag got a star for each new state.

5

Now America has 50 states.
The flag has 50 stars for 50 states.
The flag still has 13 stripes.

6

We see the flag in a lot of places.
It is a symbol for America.

7

Name: _____

I Read Closely

Look at the picture. Read the sentences.
Mark the sentence that goes with the picture.

1

    ○ People lived in colonies.

    ○ People lived in states.

2

    ○ The leaders wanted a new state.

    ○ The leaders wanted a new flag.

3

    ○ Betsy Ross was asked to sew the new flag.

    ○ People see the flag in a lot of places.

4

    ○ Now the flag has 50 stars.

    ○ Now the flag has 80 stars.

I Use New Words

Write the missing word to complete the sentence.
Then read the sentence.

1   Betsy Ross   George Washington

_____ could sew well.

2   Leaders   Colonies

_____ are where people lived.

3   people   states

America has 50 _____.

4   Betsy Ross   George Washington

_____ was a leader.

5   symbol   star

The flag is a _____ for America.

I Write About It

1 How did George Washington help get a new flag? Write about it.

_____

_____

_____

_____

_____

_____

2 How did Betsy Ross help make a new flag? Write about it.

_____

_____

_____

_____

_____

_____

American Songs and Symbols

Topic: American Songs and Symbols
Big Question: What songs and symbols tell me I'm in America?

Tie It Together

Use the script below to guide students in discussing the Big Question and what they have learned about the topic from the paired texts. Feel free to expand on these questions and responses.

Questions	Sample Responses
Think about the books you read. What is the name of the traditional song you read about?	*"My Country 'Tis of Thee" is the song we read about.*
You read about an American symbol and how it started long ago. What symbol is it?	*We read about the first American flag that was made for the 13 colonies before we had states.*
What do *My Country 'Tis of Thee* and *A Flag for America* help us think about?	*We think about freedom, our ancestors, the people who came to live in America, and the leaders who lived long ago.*
What are some other symbols of America that you saw in *My Country 'Tis of Thee?*	*The Liberty Bell and the Statue of Liberty were shown in the book "My Country 'Tis of Thee."*
In the two books, how can you tell that George Washington, Betsy Ross, and our ancestors lived a long time ago?	*Their clothes and hair look like they are from a long time ago. Also, the year that George Washington asked Betsy Ross to make the new flag was 1776.*
Our Big Question was "What songs and symbols tell me I'm in America?" How did the first book answer this question?	My Country 'Tis of Thee: *When we sing the song "My Country 'Tis of Thee," it reminds us that in America we have freedom and our beautiful land. We also have symbols such as the Statue of Liberty and the Liberty Bell, which help us think of the pilgrims, ancestors, and leaders who started our country.*
How did the second book answer it?	A Flag for America: *The flag that we have now started out with 13 stars and 13 stripes. As our country grew, our flag changed. Now the symbol of America is a flag that has 50 stars and 13 stripes.*

Name: _____

I Read and Understand

Read the sentence. Mark the best answer.

1 *My Country 'Tis of Thee* is mostly about _____.

○ how to be a pilgrim

○ a song about freedom

○ a song about a bell

2 *A Flag for America* is mostly about _____.

○ living in colonies

○ Betsy Ross

○ a new flag

3 Songs and symbols help us think about _____.

○ ancestors and freedom

○ people living in a state

○ places with new flags

4 Today, the American flag has _____.

○ 50 stars and 50 stripes

○ 13 stars and 13 stripes

○ 50 stars and 13 stripes

I Can!

> I can write about a song and a symbol
> of America.

1   Color the first American flag.

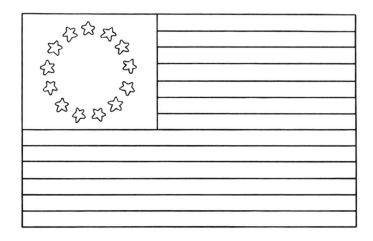

2   Write about a song and a symbol of America.
What do they mean to you?

_____

_____

_____

_____

_____

_____

Art Has Meaning

Student Objective: Students will understand that art has meaning to the artists who create it and to the people who see it.

Big Question:

What do you think when you look at art?

Topic Introduction: Explain to students that people enjoy art because it is beautiful or interesting. Point out that they also enjoy art because of what it makes them think and feel. Tell students that they will read two books that will tell about people who create art.

Paired Texts:

Assessment Materials:

Lesson Plan

1. Prepare for the Lesson

Minibook: Reproduce the minibook pages. Cut them in half and staple them together in numerical order. Distribute one minibook to each student.

Dictionary and Activity Pages: Reproduce and distribute to each student one copy of the Dictionary page and the following activity pages: I Read Closely, I Use New Words, and I Write About It.

2. Introduce the Minibook

Before the lesson, you may wish to print a picture of the *Mona Lisa.* Post it where students can see it. Then begin the lesson by directing students' attention to the picture. Tell them that they will read a book about a painting called the *Mona Lisa.* Explain that the *Mona Lisa* is one of the most famous paintings in the world.

3. Learn New Vocabulary

Guide students through the Dictionary page. Read each word aloud as you point to the picture. Have students echo you. Discuss word meanings as needed.

For the Words to Know at the bottom of the page, read each word aloud and have students echo you. Point out the following:

- The word *famous* means "a lot of people know about it."

- In this book, the word *wonder* means "a feeling of wanting to know something" or "thinking about something."

4. Read the Minibook

Lead students in a choral reading of the minibook. Then guide students in discussing what they have read. Help them identify the following:

- **Main idea**—Art makes people feel wonder; art can make people feel happy or sad.

- **Supporting details**—Artists look at the world around them to draw or paint or make something. Artists can be young or old. The *Mona Lisa* really made people wonder.

5. Read the Teacher's Complex Text

Read the Teacher's Complex Text (p. 131) as students look at the pictures in their minibooks. Before you begin reading, say:

Look at the pictures in your book as I read aloud more information about "The Wonder of Art." Look at the picture on page 1. Listen as I read.

6. Complete the Activity Pages

Guide students through completing the I Read Closely, I Use New Words, and I Write About It activities. Have students use their minibooks to help them answer questions and find information.

Teacher's Complex Text

Minibook Title Page

Minibook Page 1

People who make art are called artists. Artists can be young or old. Artists pay attention to what they see. They learn about colors and shapes and how to use them. They study how it looks when light shines on an object. Artists know that everything they see can be made into art.

Minibook Page 1

Minibook Page 2

Artists look at the world around them to get ideas. Art can be a drawing, painting, sculpture, or something else that you make.

Minibook Page 2

Minibook Page 3

Art can make people have happy or sad feelings, or make people wonder. People who look at art can be curious about what the artist was thinking or what meaning the artist wanted to show. Sometimes artists want their art to look real, but other times they want their art to show an idea or a feeling.

Minibook Page 3

Minibook Page 4

One artist really made people wonder. He lived about 500 years ago. His name was Leonardo da Vinci. He was a famous artist, but he was also an inventor and scientist.

Minibook Page 4

Minibook Page 5

Leonardo da Vinci's most famous painting is a painting of a woman, called the *Mona Lisa*. People from all over the world go to see the painting at an art museum in France. They crowd around the *Mona Lisa* to look, think, and wonder what it means.

Minibook Page 5

Minibook Page 6

People wonder why she has a little smile. They wonder what she was thinking about. She looks so real that people feel like she is looking at them. Leonardo da Vinci studied the human body, so he was able to make the people in his art look real.

Minibook Page 6

Minibook Page 7

Art can be fun and interesting. When you make art, you can show what you see, how you feel, or what you remember. Look with wonder at the works of other artists. Find details that help you feel, think, and see the world as the artists did.

Minibook Page 7

Name: _____

Dictionary

Read each word aloud.

art

artist

draw

paint

painting

world

Words to Know

around	called	famous	feel
old	show	something	still
thinking	wonder	years	young

The Wonder of Art

Name: _____

People who make art are called artists.
Artists can be young or old.

Artists look at the world around them.
They paint or draw or make something.

2

Art can make people feel happy.
Art can make people feel sad.
Art can make people wonder.

3

One artist really made people wonder.
He lived 500 years ago.
His name was Leonardo da Vinci.

4

People still wonder about his famous
painting called the *Mona Lisa*.

5

They wonder why she has a little smile.
They wonder what she is thinking about.

6

Art can be fun.
It can show how you feel.
It can show what you think.
It can show how you see the world.

7

Name: _____

I Read Closely

Look at the picture. Read the sentences.
Mark the sentence that goes with the picture.

1

○ Artists paint or draw or make something.

○ Artists run and jump.

2

○ Art can make people feel hot or cold.

○ Art can make people feel happy or sad.

3

○ Leonardo da Vinci lived 500 years ago.

○ Leonardo da Vinci lived 100 years ago.

4

○ People wonder why Mona Lisa looks sad.

○ People wonder why Mona Lisa has a little smile.

I Use New Words

Write the missing word to complete the sentence.
Then read the sentence.

1 artists   paintings

People who make art are _____.

2 think   smile

When I feel happy, I _____.

3 world   famous

The *Mona Lisa* is a _____ painting.

4 young   old

A child is _____.

5 show   wonder

Art can _____ how you feel.

Name: _____

I Write About It

1 See the *Mona Lisa* painting. Look at her eyes and her smile.
Draw a picture of yourself in the box next to her.

2 Write to tell what you are thinking about.

_____

_____

_____

_____

_____

_____

_____

Lesson Plan

1. Prepare for the Lesson

Minibook: Reproduce the minibook pages. Cut them in half and staple them together in numerical order. Distribute one minibook to each student.

Dictionary and Activity Pages: Reproduce and distribute to each student one copy of the Dictionary page and the following activity pages: I Read Closely, I Use New Words, and I Write About It.

2. Introduce the Minibook

Tell students that they will read a book about a girl who likes to draw pictures to show her feelings and to remember what she has seen and done.

3. Learn New Vocabulary

Guide students through the Dictionary page. Read each word aloud as you point to the picture. Have students echo you. Point out the following:

- In this book, the word *country* means "areas of land with trees, lakes, and large animals outside of a town."

- The word *picnic* means "a meal to be eaten outdoors."

- A *pond* is a very small lake.

For the Words to Know at the bottom of the page, read each word aloud and have students echo you. Discuss word meanings as needed.

4. Read the Minibook

Lead students in a choral reading of the minibook. Then guide students in discussing what they have read. Help them identify the following:

- **Main idea**—Sofia draws pictures to show her feelings and also to remember things she has seen and done.

- **Supporting details**—Sofia, her family, and her dog Gus went for a picnic in the country. Sofia saw hills, trees, a pond, and ducks. She and Gus ran and played.

5. Read the Teacher's Complex Text

Read the Teacher's Complex Text (p. 141) as students look at the pictures in their minibooks. Before you begin reading, say:

Look at the pictures in your book as I read aloud more information about "A Day in the Country." Look at the picture of Sofia waking up on page 1. Listen as I read.

6. Complete the Activity Pages

Guide students through completing the I Read Closely, I Use New Words, and I Write About It activities. Have students use their minibooks to help them answer questions and find information.

Teacher's Complex Text

Minibook Title Page

Minibook Page 1

I'm Sofia, and this is my dog Gus. My family lives in the city. There are a lot of tall buildings and busy streets here. Today is special, because we are going to spend the day in the country. We have been looking forward to doing this for a long time.

Minibook Page 1

Minibook Page 2

I help my mom make a picnic lunch and we put it in a basket. We put the basket in the car next to my dog Gus. I like to draw what I see, so I grab my drawing pad, pencil, box of crayons, and a ball for Gus.

Minibook Page 2

Minibook Page 3

It takes 2 hours to get there, which feels like a very long time. I need something to do, so I draw a picture of Gus and me riding in the car. My picture shows how happy we are to be on our way to the country.

Minibook Page 3

Minibook Page 4

Finally we get to the picnic spot in the country. I feel so happy when I see the green, grassy hills, huge trees, and a small duck pond. We take our picnic basket out of the car and set up our picnic.

Minibook Page 4

Minibook Page 5

The food looks so good, but I am too excited to eat much. Gus and I play ball in the green grass. Gus loves to catch the ball and bring it back to me. We run and play until we are tired.

Minibook Page 5

Minibook Page 6

Gus and I sit near the pond. We watch the ducks swim. From where we sit, we see the trees blow in the breeze. We see the hills and the blue sky. It is a beautiful sight to see!

Minibook Page 6

Minibook Page 7

At last, it is time to drive back home. Sitting in the car makes me think. I think about how great it felt to sit by the pond with Gus and look at everything around us. I draw a picture of what we saw in the country. Now I can always look at my picture and remember the fun we had!

Minibook Page 7

Dictionary

Read each word aloud.

country

draw

hills

picnic

pond

wind

Words to Know

blow	drive	excited	felt
picture	remember	today	

A Day in the Country

Name: _____

I'm Sofia, and this is my dog Gus.
Today we are going to the country!

1

We put a lot of things into the car.
We are ready to go!

2

We drive and drive.
I draw a picture of Gus and me.
We feel excited to go to the country.

3

At last, we get to the country!
We set up our picnic.
We see hills, trees, and a pond.

4

I am too happy to eat.
Gus and I play ball.
We run and play a lot.

5

Gus and I sit by the pond.
We see the ducks.
We see the trees blow in the wind.

It is time to go.
I will draw a picture of our day.
It will show what we did.
I will remember how we felt.

Name: _____

I Read Closely

Look at the picture. Read the sentences.
Mark the sentence that goes with the picture.

1

○ We drive and drive.

○ We set up our picnic.

2

○ I eat a lot.

○ Gus and I play ball.

3

○ Gus and I sit by the trees.

○ Gus and I sit by the pond.

4

○ I draw a picture to remember our day.

○ We see the trees blow in the wind.

I Use New Words

Write the missing word to complete the sentence.
Then read the sentence.

1   remember   drive

My mom can _____ the car.

2   wind   country

Trees blow in the _____.

3   pond   hills

We are going up and down the _____.

4   draw   drive

You can _____ a picture.

5   picnic   today

We ate a lot of food at our _____.

I Write About It

1 Draw a picture of Sofia doing something that made her feel happy.

2 Write a sentence that tells about your picture.

_____

_____

_____

3 Why does Sofia like to draw pictures? Write a sentence that tells about it.

_____

_____

_____

Art Has Meaning

Topic: Art Has Meaning
Big Question: What do you think when you look at art?

Tie It Together

Use the script below to guide students in discussing the Big Question and what they have learned about the topic from the paired texts. Feel free to expand on these questions and responses.

Questions	Sample Responses
Think about the books you read. What does an artist do?	*An artist is a person who makes art. An artist draws or paints or makes something.*
Do artists have to be adults?	*No, artists can be any age. You can be young or old to draw or paint or make something.*
How do you know that Leonardo da Vinci lived long ago?	*In "The Wonder of Art," it says that Leonardo da Vinci lived 500 years ago. Also, the picture of Leonardo da Vinci looks like it is from long ago.*
Why do people wonder about art?	*People wonder what the artist was thinking, and they wonder what kind of meaning the art has. For example, with the Mona Lisa, people see her little smile and wonder what she was thinking about.*
Who tells the story in *A Day in the Country*?	*Sofia tells the story. On page 1, she tells us her name, and then she calls herself "I" in the rest of the story.*
Our Big Question was "What do you think when you look at art?" How did *The Wonder of Art* help you answer this question?	The Wonder of Art: *I think about the art and if it makes me feel happy, sad, or some other feeling. I wonder what the artist was thinking about. I look for things such as a smile, objects, colors, or other details that help me understand the art. (For example: Mona Lisa looks friendly and happy. The picture looks dark and calm. Her hands are relaxed in her lap. She has a little smile. Is she thinking of something funny?)*
How did *A Day in the Country* help you answer it?	A Day in the Country: *Artists get ideas from everything around them to make art. Sofia wanted to make pictures of her special day with her family and show her happy feelings.*

Name: _____

I Read and Understand

Read the sentence. Mark the best answer.

1 An artist _____.

○ can't feel happy or sad

○ can be young, but not old

○ draws, paints, or makes something

2 Leonardo da Vinci _____.

○ painted the *Mona Lisa*

○ had a dog named Gus

○ lived ten years ago

3 People wonder why Mona Lisa has a little _____.

○ cat

○ smile

○ family

4 Who tells the story in *A Day in the Country*?

○ Gus

○ Sofia

○ Leonardo da Vinci

I Can!

> I can show how art has meaning to the artist and to the people who see it.

1 Draw a picture of a friend.
Then write a sentence that tells about the friend.

_____

_____

_____

_____

2 Draw a picture that shows you having a fun day.
Then write a sentence that tells about it.

_____

_____

People Find Solutions

Student Objective: Students will understand that people in history and in modern times have made discoveries and inventions that provide solutions for others.

Big Question: ## How can a great idea make our lives better?

Topic Introduction: Explain to students that many things we have came from someone's good ideas and hard work. Point out things around the classroom, such as a computer, a faucet, and a clock that were invented to make our lives better. Then tell students that they will read two selections: One is about child inventors, and the other is about how Ben Franklin discovered electricity.

Paired Text Selections:

Assessment Materials:

Lesson Plan

1. Prepare for the Lesson

Reproduce and distribute to each student one copy of the selection, the Dictionary page, and the following activity pages: I Read Closely, I Use New Words, and I Write About It.

2. Introduce the Selection

Tell students that in this selection, they will read about two children who used their ideas to invent something that would help people.

3. Learn New Vocabulary

Guide students through the Dictionary page. Read each word aloud as you point to the picture. Have students echo you. Point out the following:

- There are many different kinds of computers. This picture shows a laptop *computer*.

- The picture of a *heartbeat test* shows a chart of how the heart is beating.

For the Words to Know at the bottom of the page, read each word aloud and have students echo you. Point out the following:

- An *app* is a program downloaded to a computer or cellphone.

- An *invention* is something that has not been made before.

- In this selection, the word *track* means "to keep a record of something."

4. Read the Selection

Lead students in a choral reading of the selection. Then guide students in discussing what they have read. Help them identify the following:

- **Main idea**—Two students made inventions that help people.

- **Supporting details**—Catherine Wong invented a heartbeat test that could be done on a cellphone, and Daniel Chao invented a way to keep track of reading minutes on a computer or cellphone.

5. Read the Teacher's Complex Text

Read the Teacher's Complex Text (p. 155) as students look at the pictures in their selections. Before you begin reading, say:

Look at the pictures in your selection as I read aloud more information about "Ideas and Inventions." Look at the picture on page 1. Listen as I read.

6. Complete the Activity Pages

Guide students through completing the I Read Closely, I Use New Words, and I Write About It activities. Have students use the selection to help them answer questions and find information.

Teacher's Complex Text

Some people are very curious and have a lot of ideas. They use their ideas to think, research, plan, and make new inventions. Inventors think about what people need, and then make something that will be helpful. Many inventors find a solution for a problem.

Catherine Wong was a 17-year-old high school student who loved science. She noticed that many people have heart problems. Sometimes the heart doctor they need is far away. Catherine also noticed that most people (especially adults) have cellphones. Knowing these things gave her an idea. Catherine made a tiny tool that could fit on a cellphone. The tool does a heartbeat test with a cellphone. The test shows the heartbeat pattern on the phone screen. Then it can be sent to the doctor. The doctor can tell if someone's heart is working well or if they need help. People had a problem and Catherine found a solution.

Daniel Chao was a 10-year-old fifth grader. He had to do reading homework every day. He had to write on a calendar the number of minutes he read. Every month, he had to take his calendar to his teacher. Daniel thought there must be an easier way. He knew that a lot of other students had to keep track of reading minutes, too. Daniel had an idea. He made a program, or app, that can be used on a computer or on a cellphone. Students can use the app to keep track of how much time they read. Then it can be sent to the teacher's computer. The teacher can check to see how many minutes a student reads each month.

Catherine and Daniel had good ideas. It wasn't easy, but they worked hard and made their ideas into inventions. Their inventions help people.

student selection, pg. 157

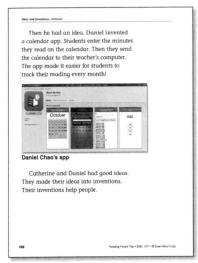

student selection, pg. 158

Dictionary

Read each word aloud.

calendar

cellphone

computer

doctor

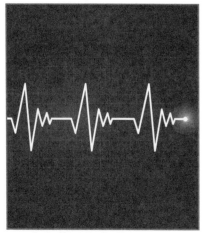

heartbeat test

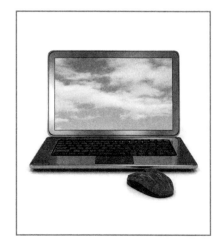

teacher

Words to Know

app	easier	enter	far
heart	homework	idea	invention
minutes	month	reading	students
track	years		

Name: _____

Ideas and Inventions

Some people have a lot of ideas. They use their ideas to make inventions. Inventions can help people.

Catherine Wong was 17 years old. She saw that many people need a heart doctor. Some doctors are far away. Catherine had an idea. Most people have a cellphone. She invented a way to do a heartbeat test on a cellphone. The test can be sent to the doctor. Then the doctor looks at it. It shows if your heartbeat is good. Catherine's invention will help people.

Catherine Wong

Daniel Chao was 10 years old. He had reading homework every day. He had to write on a calendar how many minutes he read. Every month he had to take it to his teacher. Daniel wanted to think of an easier way.

Then he had an idea. Daniel invented a calendar app. Students enter the minutes they read on the calendar. Then they send the calendar to their teacher's computer. The app made it easier for students to track their reading every month!

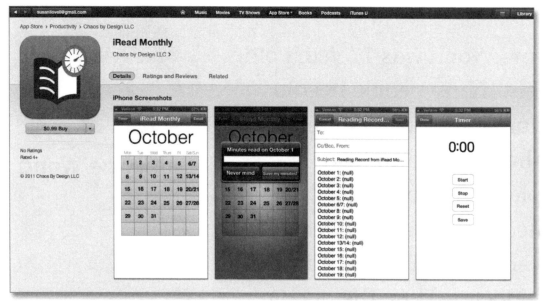

Daniel Chao's app

Catherine and Daniel had good ideas. They made their ideas into inventions. Their inventions help people.

Name: _____

I Read Closely

Look at the picture. Read the sentences.
Mark the sentence that goes with the picture.

1

   ○ Catherine Wong was 17 years old.

   ○ Catherine Wong was 27 years old.

2

   ○ Most people have a cellphone.

   ○ Most people have a test.

3

   ○ Daniel Chao had to write down how many minutes he read.

   ○ Daniel Chao did not have to do reading homework.

4

   ○ A lot of students use a cellphone.

   ○ A lot of students use a computer.

I Use New Words

Write the missing word to complete the sentence.
Then read the sentence.

1   idea   app

You need an _____ to make an invention.

2   month   homework

Do your _____ after school.

3   heartbeat   track

A doctor wants to see a _____ test.

4   teacher   heart

Your _____ needs to see your homework.

5   student   computer

An app works on a _____.

I Write About It

1 Draw a picture of the invention that helps people stay well.
Write a sentence about it.

2 Draw a picture of the invention that helps students do homework.
Write a sentence about it.

Lesson Plan

1. Prepare for the Lesson

Reproduce and distribute to each student one copy of the selection, the Dictionary page, and the following activity pages: I Read Closely, I Use New Words, and I Write About It.

2. Introduce the Selection

Direct students' attention to a picture of Benjamin Franklin. Tell students that in this selection, they will read about Ben Franklin, who is famous for many things he did in the 1700s. Point out that there are often different stories and details about what really happened long ago. Explain to students that in this selection, they will read about one of Ben Franklin's discoveries.

3. Learn New Vocabulary

Guide students through the Dictionary page. Read each word aloud as you point to the picture. Have students echo you. Point out the following:

- *Electricity* is a form of energy that we use to power lamps, heat houses, and run computers and many other things we use.

For the Words to Know at the bottom of the page, read each word aloud and have students echo you. Point out the following:

- The word *discover* means "to find out about something before anyone else." (Also discuss *discovery* and *discovered*.)

- The word *spark* means "a small piece of burning material that comes from a fire."

4. Read the Selection

Lead students in a choral reading of the selection. Then guide students in discussing what they have read. Help them identify the following:

- **Main idea**—Ben Franklin discovered electricity.

- **Supporting details**—Ben flew a kite in the rain. Electricity from the lightning went down the string and made sparks on the key.

5. Read the Teacher's Complex Text

Read the Teacher's Complex Text (p. 163) as students look at the pictures in their selections. Before you begin reading, say:

Look at the pictures in your selection as I read aloud more information about "Ben Franklin." Look at the picture on page 1. Listen as I read.

6. Complete the Activity Pages

Guide students through completing the I Read Closely, I Use New Words, and I Write About It activities. Have students use the selection to help them answer questions and find information.

Teacher's Complex Text

Ben Franklin was born in 1706. There were 17 children in his family. When Ben was growing up, people had to pay for school. Ben's family could only afford to send him to school for 2 years. Even so, Ben loved to read. He was very curious and had a lot of ideas.

Ben wanted to help people and make their lives more comfortable. People living at that time didn't have electricity. They didn't know where electricity came from or how it could help them. People had to use candles for light and fireplaces to warm their homes. Neither worked very well, and people wanted an easier way to get light and heat.

Ben was very curious about lightning. He wanted to know more about it and planned ways to experiment, or find out more about it. He had an idea that lightning might be electricity, but he had to prove whether or not his idea was true. Ben also knew that lightning could be dangerous, if he was not careful.

One story says that in 1752, Ben made a kite. He put a key on the kite string. He waited for a thunderstorm to come. When it started to rain, he flew the kite in the air and tied the string to the ground. Then he waited in a safe place and watched for the lightning to come.

The lightning struck the kite. Electricity went down the wet kite string. Ben saw sparks fly from the key. Then he knew for sure that lightning was electricity!

Ben Franklin shared his discovery with others. He wanted other people to learn about electricity so that everyone could use it. Now people have heat and light in their homes and communities. People use electricity to have light at night and to warm their homes. They can also use it to listen to music, cook food, work on a computer, watch TV, and do so many other things.

student selection, pg. 165

student selection, pg. 166

Name: _____

Dictionary

Read each word aloud.

Ben Franklin

kite

lightning

sparks

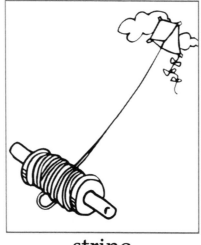

string

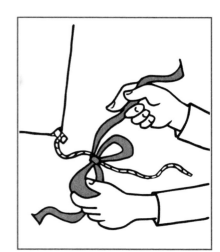

tied

Words to Know

born	discovery	electricity	ground
heat	ideas	knew	light
needed	people	rain	read

Reading Paired Text • EMC 1371 • © Evan-Moor Corp.

Ben Franklin

Ben Franklin was born in 1706.
He liked to read.
Ben had a lot of ideas.

Ben wanted to help people.
People needed light and heat.
People didn't have electricity.

Ben wanted to know about lightning.
He wanted to find out if lightning
    was electricity.

In 1752, Ben made a kite.
He put a key on the kite string.
The rain and lightning came.
He let the kite go up.
He tied the kite string to the ground.

Electricity went down the wet
    kite string.
Ben saw sparks on the key.
Then he knew that lightning
    is electricity.

Ben told people about his discovery.
Now people have heat and light.
Now people use electricity in
    a lot of ways.

Name: _____

I Read Closely

Look at the picture. Read the sentences.
Mark the sentence that goes with the picture.

1

○ Ben Franklin was born
in 1706.

○ Ben Franklin was born
in 1906.

2

○ Ben liked to play.

○ Ben liked to read.

3

○ Ben wanted to find out if
lightning was electricity.

○ Ben wanted to find out if
lightning was rain.

4

○ In 1752, Ben made a kite.

○ In 1752, Ben made a string.

I Use New Words

Write the missing word to complete the sentence.
Then read the sentence.

1   electricity   discovery

We use _____ for light and heat.

2   heat   ground

I walk on the _____.

3   string   rain

A kite has a _____ tied to it.

4   ideas   lightning

Out in the rain, we saw _____.

5   kite   knew

You can fly a _____.

I Write About It

1 Draw a picture of Ben's discovery.

2 Write about Ben's discovery.

_____

_____

_____

_____

_____

Word Bank

electricity   lightning   rain   sparks

People Find Solutions

Topic: People Find Solutions
Big Question: How can a great idea make our lives better?

Tie It Together

Use the script below to guide students in discussing the Big Question and what they have learned about the topic from the paired selections. Feel free to expand on these questions and responses.

Questions	Sample Responses
Think about the selections you read. What inventions or discoveries do they tell about?	*A cellphone heartbeat test, a way to track reading minutes on a computer, and electricity were described in the selections.*
What does someone need to invent or discover something?	*People need an idea. It can be an idea that will help solve a problem or make life better.*
Do you have to be an adult to invent or discover something?	*No, you do not have to be an adult to have a great idea or make an invention. Catherine Wong was 17 years old, and Daniel Chao was 10.*
In the selections you read, who made a discovery a long time ago?	*Ben Franklin*
What did he discover, and how did he do it?	*Ben Franklin wanted to know about lightning. He tied a key to a kite string. Then he flew the kite in a storm. Ben saw sparks on the key. Then Ben Franklin knew that lightning is electricity.*
Do you think Ben Franklin's discovery about electricity helped people have other ideas about new inventions?	*After Ben Franklin discovered electricity, other people could think of ways to use the electricity. For example, lamps, streetlights, televisions, radios, computers, and cellphones all need electricity to work.*
Our Big Question was "How can a great idea make our lives better?" How did Ideas and Inventions answer this question?	Ideas and Inventions: *A great idea can help people stay healthy, as with the heartbeat test. A great idea can make something easier, such as tracking reading minutes on a computer.*
How did Ben Franklin answer it?	Ben Franklin: *A great discovery can make life easier. Knowing about electricity helped people think of ideas for inventing ways to use it, such as lamps, televisions, computers, etc.*

I Read and Understand

Read the sentence. Mark the best answer.

1 Ben Franklin discovered ____.

○ electricity

○ a computer

○ a cellphone

2 Catherine Wong made ____ to do on a cellphone.

○ a kite

○ homework

○ a heartbeat test

3 Daniel Chao's invention helps keep track of ____.

○ heartbeat tests

○ reading minutes

○ ways people use electricity

4 Catherine Wong, Daniel Chao, and Ben Franklin ____.

○ had ideas to make our lives better

○ had a great way to make a kite

○ gave up on their ideas

I Can!

I can tell how an idea helped people make an invention or discovery.

Think about what you read. Write about Catherine Wong, Daniel Chao, and Ben Franklin. Tell how their ideas helped them make an invention or discovery.

_____

_____

_____

_____

_____

_____

_____

_____

Word Bank

app	doctor	electricity
heartbeat test	kite	lightning
minutes	reading homework	teacher

Answer Key

TE = Teacher's Edition
SB = Student Book

My Skeletal System

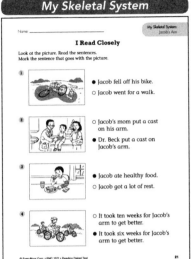

TE Page 21 / SB Page 12

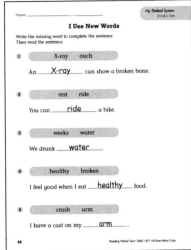

TE Page 22 / SB Page 13

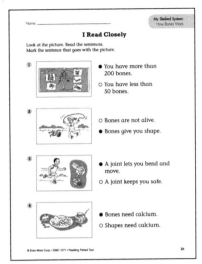

TE Page 31 / SB Page 24

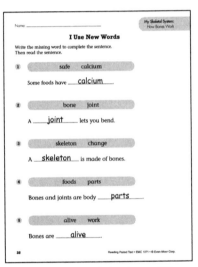

TE Page 32 / SB Page 25

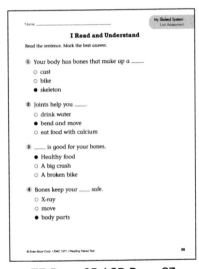

TE Page 35 / SB Page 27

Earth's Moon and Sun

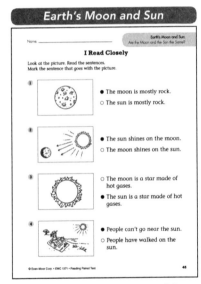

TE Page 45 / SB Page 38

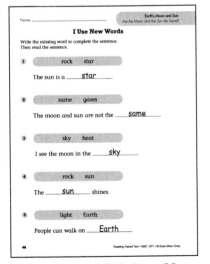

TE Page 46 / SB Page 39

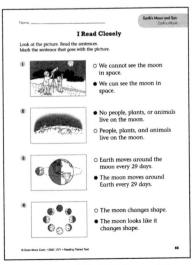

TE Page 55 / SB Page 50

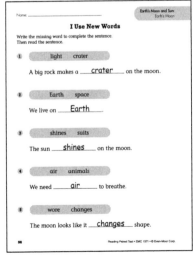

TE Page 56 / SB Page 51

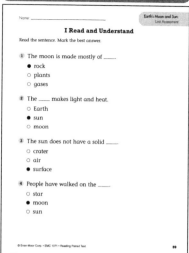

Name: _____

Earth's Moon and Sun:
Unit Assessment

I Read and Understand

Read the sentence. Mark the best answer.

1 The moon is made mostly of ____.
- ● rock
- ○ plants
- ○ gases

2 The ____ makes light and heat.
- ○ Earth
- ● sun
- ○ moon

3 The sun does not have a solid ____.
- ○ crater
- ○ air
- ● surface

4 People have walked on the ____.
- ○ star
- ● moon
- ○ sun

© Evan-Moor Corp. • EMC 1371 • Reading Paired Text   59

TE Page 59 / SB Page 53

Name: _____

Everything Is Made of Matter:
What Is Matter?

I Read Closely

Look at the picture. Read the sentences.
Mark the sentence that goes with the picture.

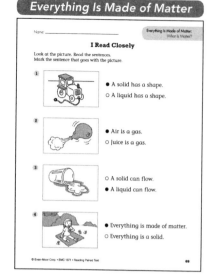

1
- ● A solid has a shape.
- ○ A liquid has a shape.

2
- ● Air is a gas.
- ○ Juice is a gas.

3
- ○ A solid can flow.
- ● A liquid can flow.

4
- ● Everything is made of matter.
- ○ Everything is a solid.

© Evan-Moor Corp. • EMC 1371 • Reading Paired Text   69

TE Page 69 / SB Page 64

Name: _____

Everything Is Made of Matter:
What Is Matter?

I Use New Words

Write the missing word to complete the sentence.
Then read the sentence.

1 air   toys

My ____toys____ are solids.

2 flow   solid

Water can ____flow____.

3 water   matter

Everything is made of ____matter____.

4 solid   shape

Juice has no ____shape____.

5 liquid   gas

Air is a ____gas____.

70   Reading Paired Text • EMC 1371 • © Evan-Moor Corp.

TE Page 70 / SB Page 65

Name: _____

Everything Is Made of Matter:
Wonderful Water

I Read Closely

Look at the picture. Read the sentences.
Mark the sentence that goes with the picture.

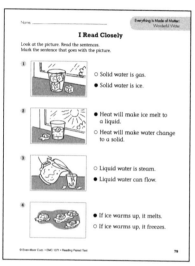

1
- ○ Solid water is gas.
- ● Solid water is ice.

2
- ● Heat will make ice melt to a liquid.
- ○ Heat will make water change to a solid.

3
- ○ Liquid water is steam.
- ● Liquid water can flow.

4
- ● If ice warms up, it melts.
- ○ If ice warms up, it freezes.

© Evan-Moor Corp. • EMC 1371 • Reading Paired Text   79

TE Page 79 / SB Page 76

Name: _____

Everything Is Made of Matter:
Wonderful Water

I Use New Words

Write the missing word to complete the sentence.
Then read the sentence.

1 glass   think

I can put water in a ____glass____.

2 heat   gas

Steam is a ____gas____.

3 solid   liquid

Water that freezes turns into a ____solid____.

4 freeze   flow

If you spill water, it will ____flow____.

5 melt   splash

Ice will ____melt____ in the sun.

80   Reading Paired Text • EMC 1371 • © Evan-Moor Corp.

TE Page 80 / SB Page 77

Name: _____

Everything Is Made of Matter:
Unit Assessment

I Read and Understand

Read the sentence. Mark the best answer.

1 The forms of matter are ____.
- ○ solid, big, liquid
- ● solid, liquid, gas
- ○ liquid, gas, hot

2 Ice, toys, and books are ____.
- ● solids
- ○ liquids
- ○ gases

3 Steam is water that changed to a ____.
- ● gas
- ○ liquid
- ○ matter

4 Everything around us is made of ____.
- ○ gas
- ○ solids
- ● matter

© Evan-Moor Corp. • EMC 1371 • Reading Paired Text   83

TE Page 83 / SB Page 79

Name: _____

Animal Classification:
Goats

I Read Closely

Look at the picture. Read the sentences.
Mark the sentence that goes with the picture.

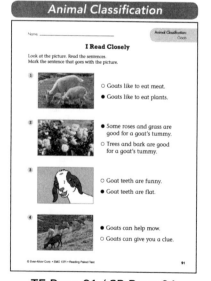

1
- ○ Goats like to eat meat.
- ● Goats like to eat plants.

2
- ● Some roses and grass are good for a goat's tummy.
- ○ Trees and bark are good for a goat's tummy.

3
- ○ Goat teeth are funny.
- ● Goat teeth are flat.

4
- ● Goats can help mow.
- ○ Goats can give you a clue.

© Evan-Moor Corp. • EMC 1371 • Reading Paired Text   91

TE Page 91 / SB Page 84

Name: _____

Animal Classification:
Goats

I Use New Words

Write the missing word to complete the sentence.
Then read the sentence.

1 clue   crunch

A ____clue____ helps you find out.

2 think   mow

To cut the grass is to ____mow____.

3 grind   herd

A lot of goats is a ____herd____.

4 yummy   tummy

A food you like to eat is ____yummy____.

5 meat   chew

I ____chew____ my food when I eat.

92   Reading Paired Text • EMC 1371 • © Evan-Moor Corp.

TE Page 92 / SB Page 85

Name: _____

Animal Classification:
Wild About Food

I Read Closely

Look at the picture. Read the sentences.
Mark the sentence that goes with the picture.

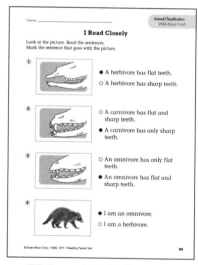

1
- ● A herbivore has flat teeth.
- ○ A herbivore has sharp teeth.

2
- ○ A carnivore has flat and sharp teeth.
- ● A carnivore has only sharp teeth.

3
- ○ An omnivore has only flat teeth.
- ● An omnivore has flat and sharp teeth.

4
- ● I am an omnivore.
- ○ I am a herbivore.

© Evan-Moor Corp. • EMC 1371 • Reading Paired Text   99

TE Page 99 / SB Page 90

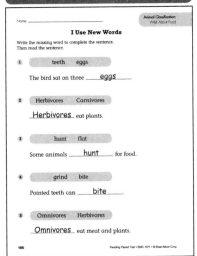

I Use New Words

Write the missing word to complete the sentence.
Then read the sentence.

① teeth   eggs

The bird sat on three __eggs__.

② Herbivores   Carnivores

__Herbivores__ eat plants.

③ hunt   flat

Some animals __hunt__ for food.

④ grind   bite

Pointed teeth can __bite__.

⑤ Omnivores   Herbivores

__Omnivores__ eat meat and plants.

TE Page 100 / SB Page 91

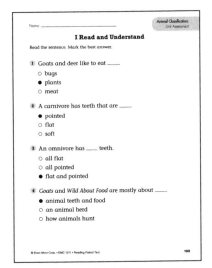

I Read and Understand

Read the sentence. Mark the best answer.

① Goats and deer like to eat ____.
○ bugs
● plants
○ meat

② A carnivore has teeth that are ____.
● pointed
○ flat
○ soft

③ An omnivore has ____ teeth.
○ all flat
○ all pointed
● flat and pointed

④ *Goats* and *Wild About Food* are mostly about ____.
● animal teeth and food
○ an animal herd
○ how animals hunt

TE Page 103 / SB Page 93

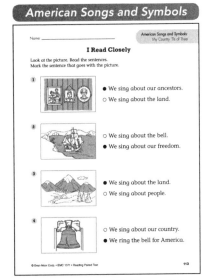

I Read Closely

Look at the picture. Read the sentences.
Mark the sentence that goes with the picture.

① ● We sing about our ancestors.
○ We sing about the land.

② ○ We sing about the bell.
● We sing about our freedom.

③ ● We sing about the land.
○ We sing about people.

④ ○ We sing about our country.
● We ring the bell for America.

TE Page 113 / SB Page 104

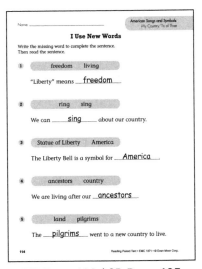

I Use New Words

Write the missing word to complete the sentence.
Then read the sentence.

① freedom   living

"Liberty" means __freedom__.

② ring   sing

We can __sing__ about our country.

③ Statue of Liberty   America

The Liberty Bell is a symbol for __America__.

④ ancestors   country

We are living after our __ancestors__.

⑤ land   pilgrims

The __pilgrims__ went to a new country to live.

TE Page 114 / SB Page 105

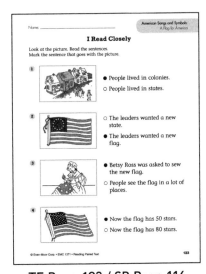

I Read Closely

Look at the picture. Read the sentences.
Mark the sentence that goes with the picture.

① ● People lived in colonies.
○ People lived in states.

② ○ The leaders wanted a new state.
● The leaders wanted a new flag.

③ ● Betsy Ross was asked to sew the new flag.
○ People see the flag in a lot of places.

④ ● Now the flag has 50 stars.
○ Now the flag has 80 stars.

TE Page 123 / SB Page 116

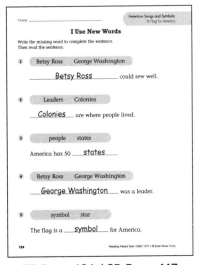

I Use New Words

Write the missing word to complete the sentence.
Then read the sentence.

① Betsy Ross   George Washington

__Betsy Ross__ could sew well.

② Leaders   Colonies

__Colonies__ are where people lived.

③ people   states

America has 50 __states__.

④ Betsy Ross   George Washington

__George Washington__ was a leader.

⑤ symbol   star

The flag is a __symbol__ for America.

TE Page 124 / SB Page 117

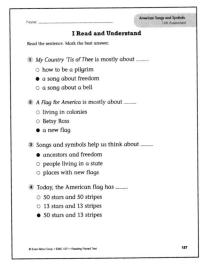

I Read and Understand

Read the sentence. Mark the best answer.

① *My Country 'Tis of Thee* is mostly about ____.
○ how to be a pilgrim
● a song about freedom
○ a song about a bell

② *A Flag for America* is mostly about ____.
○ living in colonies
○ Betsy Ross
● a new flag

③ Songs and symbols help us think about ____.
● ancestors and freedom
○ people living in a state
○ places with new flags

④ Today, the American flag has ____.
○ 50 stars and 50 stripes
○ 13 stars and 13 stripes
● 50 stars and 13 stripes

TE Page 127 / SB Page 119

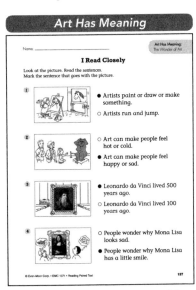

I Read Closely

Look at the picture. Read the sentences.
Mark the sentence that goes with the picture.

① ● Artists paint or draw or make something.
○ Artists run and jump.

② ○ Art can make people feel hot or cold.
● Art can make people feel happy or sad.

③ ● Leonardo da Vinci lived 500 years ago.
○ Leonardo da Vinci lived 100 years ago.

④ ○ People wonder why Mona Lisa looks sad.
● People wonder why Mona Lisa has a little smile.

TE Page 137 / SB Page 130

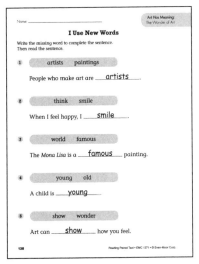

I Use New Words

Write the missing word to complete the sentence.
Then read the sentence.

① artists   paintings

People who make art are __artists__.

② think   smile

When I feel happy, I __smile__.

③ world   famous

The *Mona Lisa* is a __famous__ painting.

④ young   old

A child is __young__.

⑤ show   wonder

Art can __show__ how you feel.

TE Page 138 / SB Page 131

I Read Closely

Look at the picture. Read the sentences.
Mark the sentence that goes with the picture.

1. ○ We drive and drive.
   ● We set up our picnic.

2. ○ I eat a lot.
   ● Gus and I play ball.

3. ○ Gus and I sit by the trees.
   ● Gus and I sit by the pond.

4. ● I draw a picture to remember our day.
   ○ We see the trees blow in the wind.

TE Page 147 / SB Page 142

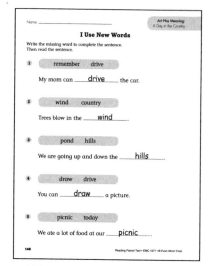

I Use New Words

Write the missing word to complete the sentence.
Then read the sentence.

1. remember   drive
   My mom can ___drive___ the car.

2. wind   country
   Trees blow in the ___wind___.

3. pond   hills
   We are going up and down the ___hills___.

4. draw   drive
   You can ___draw___ a picture.

5. picnic   today
   We ate a lot of food at our ___picnic___.

TE Page 148 / SB Page 143

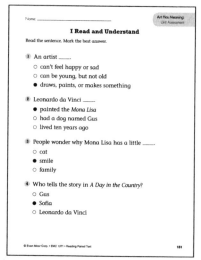

I Read and Understand

Read the sentence. Mark the best answer.

1. An artist ___.
   ○ can't feel happy or sad
   ○ can be young, but not old
   ● draws, paints, or makes something

2. Leonardo da Vinci ___.
   ● painted the *Mona Lisa*
   ○ had a dog named Gus
   ○ lived ten years ago

3. People wonder why Mona Lisa has a little ___.
   ○ cat
   ● smile
   ○ family

4. Who tells the story in *A Day in the Country*?
   ○ Gus
   ● Sofia
   ○ Leonardo da Vinci

TE Page 151 / SB Page 145

People Find Solutions

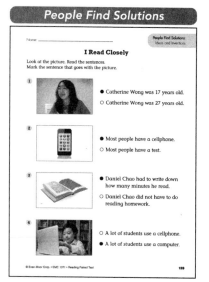

I Read Closely

Look at the picture. Read the sentences.
Mark the sentence that goes with the picture.

1. ● Catherine Wong was 17 years old.
   ○ Catherine Wong was 27 years old.

2. ● Most people have a cellphone.
   ○ Most people have a test.

3. ● Daniel Chao had to write down how many minutes he read.
   ○ Daniel Chao did not have to do reading homework.

4. ○ A lot of students use a cellphone.
   ● A lot of students use a computer.

TE Page 159 / SB Page 150

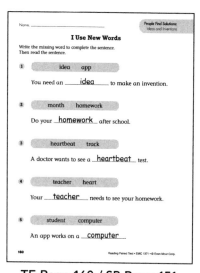

I Use New Words

Write the missing word to complete the sentence.
Then read the sentence.

1. idea   app
   You need an ___idea___ to make an invention.

2. month   homework
   Do your ___homework___ after school.

3. heartbeat   track
   A doctor wants to see a ___heartbeat___ test.

4. teacher   heart
   Your ___teacher___ needs to see your homework.

5. student   computer
   An app works on a ___computer___.

TE Page 160 / SB Page 151

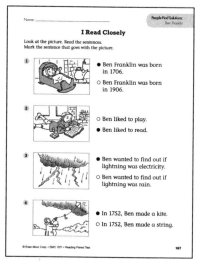

I Read Closely

Look at the picture. Read the sentences.
Mark the sentence that goes with the picture.

1. ● Ben Franklin was born in 1706.
   ○ Ben Franklin was born in 1906.

2. ○ Ben liked to play.
   ● Ben liked to read.

3. ● Ben wanted to find out if lightning was electricity.
   ○ Ben wanted to find out if lightning was rain.

4. ● In 1752, Ben made a kite.
   ○ In 1752, Ben made a string.

TE Page 167 / SB Page 156

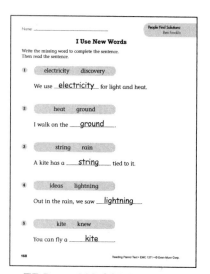

I Use New Words

Write the missing word to complete the sentence.
Then read the sentence.

1. electricity   discovery
   We use ___electricity___ for light and heat.

2. heat   ground
   I walk on the ___ground___.

3. string   rain
   A kite has a ___string___ tied to it.

4. ideas   lightning
   Out in the rain, we saw ___lightning___.

5. kite   knew
   You can fly a ___kite___.

TE Page 168 / SB Page 157

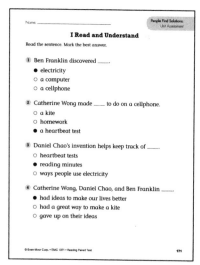

I Read and Understand

Read the sentence. Mark the best answer.

1. Ben Franklin discovered ___.
   ● electricity
   ○ a computer
   ○ a cellphone

2. Catherine Wong made ___ to do on a cellphone.
   ○ a kite
   ○ homework
   ● a heartbeat test

3. Daniel Chao's invention helps keep track of ___.
   ○ heartbeat tests
   ● reading minutes
   ○ ways people use electricity

4. Catherine Wong, Daniel Chao, and Ben Franklin ___.
   ● had ideas to make our lives better
   ○ had a great way to make a kite
   ○ gave up on their ideas

TE Page 171 / SB Page 159